Double
WEDDING RING
Quilts

COMING FULL CIRCLE

American Quilter's Society

P. O. Box 3290 • Paducah, KY 42002-3290
www.AQSquilt.com

Located in Paducah, Kentucky, the American Quilter's Society (AQS) is dedicated to promoting the accomplishments of today's quilters. Through its publications and events, AQS strives to honor today's quiltmakers and their work and to inspire future creativity and innovation in quiltmaking.

Editor: Jane Townswick
Technical Editor: Helen Squire
Graphic Design: Lynda Smith
Cover Design: Michael Buckingham
Photography: Charles R. Lynch

Library of Congress Cataloging-in-Publication Data
Stein, Susan (Susan L.).
    Double wedding ring quilts : coming full circle / by Susan Stein.
        p. cm.
     ISBN 1-57432-771-2
   1. Patchwork--Patterns. 2. Double wedding ring quilts. 3. Wall
hangings. 4. Fancy work. I. Title.
   TT835 .S72 2001
    746.46'041--dc21
                            2001002279

Additional copies of this book may be ordered from the American Quilter's Society, PO Box 3290, Paducah, KY 42002-3290, or online at www.AQSquilt.com.

Dedication

To John, for all his love and support over the past 35 years and for loving trains as much as I love quilts so I can indulge my passion without guilt.

To Sharon Hultgren, mentor, good friend, and supporter in the quilting world and beyond.

To Dawn Hall, without whose Cherrywood Fabrics I never would have made 55 Double Wedding Rings and countless other colorful quilts.

Contents

Introduction

Traditional Double Wedding Ring quilts are perennial favorites that bring smiles to the faces of everyone who sees them. The fluid curves in this pattern move the viewer's eye around a quilt top in a more pleasing way than do many straight-lined geometric patterns. What makes Double Wedding Ring quilts so much fun to make is the variety of shapes in the pattern and the different sizes of the pieces which allow you to experiment with a multitude of creative embellishments, and design variations., and fabric use.

The wallhangings in this book are small, which offers several advantages. First, it takes less fabric to make a smaller quilt; you can use one yard of a smashing hand-dyed or imported fabric or a bundle of hand-dyed fat quarters and a yard of commercial background fabric for making up to twelve rings. You can also add one more fabric, if you wish to border the rings. Second, you can finish small projects more quickly than large ones, which gives you more time for making more quilts and experimenting with innovative techniques. I also like the ease of handling a small quilt for machine quilting. And finally, wall quilts make superb gifts for very special friends and family members.

Think of the Double Wedding Ring pattern as a blank canvas for exploring new ways to lead the viewer's eye across the surface of a quilt, to suggest symbolic meanings, and to create complex graphic designs. The open background areas inside the "rings" are the perfect place to try out the surface designs like grid strips and raw-edged piecing, and embellishment techniques shown in these projects, such as burned-silk appliqué, crazy quilting, and layered chenille. Using landscape, plaid, and striped fabrics can also give a Wedding Ring quilt a very distinctive personality as can using a time-tested block such as Nine-Patch. Look for each project's special technique listed below its photograph.

These projects are a jumping-off place. They are not difficult, and after you make one, you're likely to find yourself addicted to them. There are endless possibilities for expanding the rings, distorting them, or superimposing them on other patterns. Let your imagination roam and have fun as you investigate the limitless design potential in the Double Wedding Ring pattern.

General Guidelines

Use the following chart and general guidelines for cutting out the pieces for any Double Wedding Ring quilt (see layout on page 8) with precision. All the quilts in the book were made with a 15" finished size ring (pattern on pages 91–93), and fabrics and supplies listed for each project are for that size.

Cutting Chart for Multiple Rings

Number of pieces needed for a Double Wedding Ring quilt that contains from three to twelve rings.

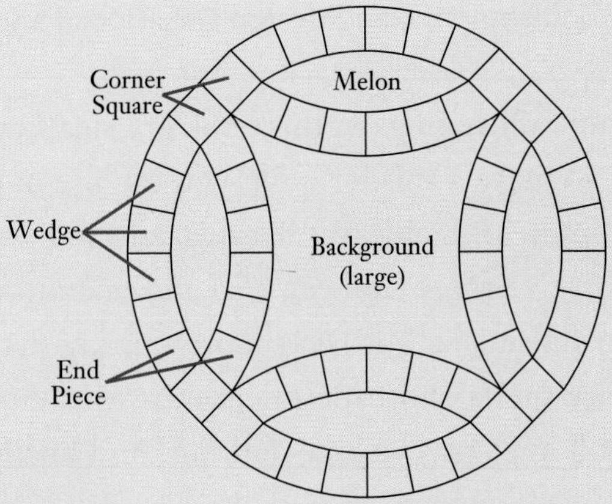

Diagram labels: Corner Square, Melon, Wedge, Background (large), End Piece

Three Rings
Cut 20 *wedges* from each of four fabrics

Cut 20 *end pieces* from each of two fabrics

Cut 10 *corner squares* from each of two fabrics

Cut 10 *melons* from background fabric

Cut   3 *background* large pieces

Five Rings
Cut 32 *wedges* from each of four fabrics

Cut 32 *end pieces* from each of two fabrics

Cut 16 *corner squares* from each of two fabrics

Cut 16 *melons* from background fabric

Cut   5 *background* large pieces

Six Rings
Cut 34 *wedges* from each of four fabrics

Cut 34 *end pieces* from each of two fabrics

Cut 17 *corner squares* from each of two fabrics

Cut 17 *melons* from background fabric

Cut   6 *background* large pieces

Eight Rings
Cut 44 *wedges* from each of four fabrics

Cut 44 *end pieces* from each of two fabrics

Cut 22 *corner squares* from each of two fabrics

Cut 22 *melons* from background fabric

Cut   8 *background* large pieces

Nine Rings
Cut 48 *wedges* from each of four fabrics

Cut 48 *end pieces* from each of two fabrics

Cut 24 *corner squares* from each of two fabrics

Cut 24 *melons* from background fabric

Cut   9 *background* large pieces

Twelve Rings
Cut 62 *wedges* from each of four fabrics

Cut 62 *end pieces* from each of two fabrics

Cut 31 *corner squares* from each of two fabrics

Cut 31 *melons* from background fabric

Cut 12 *background* large pieces

Double Wedding Ring Quilts: Coming Full Circle – Susan L. Stein

Templates vs. Patterns There are many different types of Double Wedding Ring template sets and patterns available in today's market. I recommend that you use a good set of acrylic templates to speed up the cutting process and ensure the highest degree of piecing accuracy. For my preferences in acrylic templates, see Resources, page 94-95. For a printed pattern for a 15" Double Wedding Ring, see pages 92-93.

Pre-treating Fabrics Whether to prewash fabrics or not depends on your own preferences and on the way you plan to launder the finished quilt. I suggest rinsing commercial fabrics in the washer, machine drying them, and checking the water for bleeding. If this occurs, you can rinse the fabric a second time. I do not recommend prewashing artist's hand-dyed fabrics, because they have already been washed several times by the time you purchase them. I think that prewashing commercial fabrics helps to shrink them a bit and make the grain of the fabric a little straighter.

Press for Success Before you begin cutting out any of the pieces for a Double Wedding ring quilt, press your fabrics thoroughly. I use a lot of steam to make sure that the fabrics will be perfectly smooth. If

More Double Wedding Ring Suggestions

You can also make your own Double Wedding Ring *templates*, using a printed pattern and template plastic. If you do this, be sure to include ¼" seam allowances in your templates and plan on test-sewing a couple of rings to make sure they will turn out accurately.

Cut a tiny strip of each fabric and tape it to an index card in the order you plan to piece the arcs for your Double Wedding Rings. Keep it where you can refer to it often as you machine piece the rings.

As you *cut* the wedges, end pieces, and corner squares for your quilt, lay them in a small box, so they are all in order when you are ready to machine piece.

A scant ¼" *seam allowance* usually works well for most people, especially when using hand-dyed fabrics, which can be thicker than commercially printed broadcloth.

To speed up the *cutting process* for the end pieces, cut your fabrics along the fold. Layer them so that both pieces of one fabric lie in one direction and both pieces of the second fabric lie in the opposite direction.

Another creative way to use *fabric* in corner squares is to feature one fabric at each end of all the horizontal melons, and use the other fabric for all of the corner squares of the vertical melons. Antique Double Wedding Rings often feature this approach.

When you want to make a quilt quickly, try using a single-fabric *arc template* that eliminates both the wedges and the end pieces. (See Resources, page 92, Templates, for my preferences.) This means that corner squares are the only small pieces you need to cut for this type of Double Wedding Ring quilt.

After *cutting* one pair of end pieces, you can align the straight edge of the template with the cut edge of the fabric and cut the next set of end pieces. This method will allow you to conserve both fabric and cutting time.

If your machine tends to pucker the fabric when you do close *stitching*, place blank newsprint or tracing paper under the layers as you stitch, for a smoother flow and finished appearance. Rip off the paper after the stitching is completed.

you do not like to put water into your iron, you can mist the fabrics with water before pressing them. After you finish pressing each piece of fabric, lay it out on a cutting mat. Place the remaining fabrics in single layers, on top. Line up the selvages so that the grain lines of the fabrics are straight and consistent.

Rotary Cutting Tips

- Use a size 28mm rotary cutter as you cut the pieces for your quilt, so that the blade will "hug" the curves of the acrylic templates and make precise cuts.
- Use a rotary cutter that has few bulky screws or safety devices along the sides of the blade, which can obscure your view as you cut. Being able to see clearly makes it easier to keep the blade absolutely tight to the side of a curved template.
- Do a few test-cuts to make sure that your rotary cutter's blade is sharp enough to cut curved pieces accurately.
- Close the safety cover on the rotary cutter as soon as you finish making each cut, so you won't nick your fingers.
- To avoid straining your back, cut at a height that is comfortable for you. I recommend standing up, which helps you get the best leverage on the rotary-cutter blade and gives you the best view of all the edges of the templates.
- To make acrylic templates "non-slip," attach self-adhesive sandpaper dots to the corners of all of the acrylic templates you plan to use. Cutting accuracy is

lost if your templates move even the slightest bit, so make sure your templates grip the fabric well. You can also add sandpaper dots to the center areas of larger templates.

Cutting a Double Wedding Ring

The parts that make up the arcs, and ultimately the rings, of a Double Wedding Ring pattern include the *wedges*, *end pieces*, and *corner squares*. The *background* area consists of smaller, *melon-shaped* pieces and larger pieces that appear to be behind the rings. Photographs that illustrate cutting, sewing, and positioning of these pieces and that show quilting and embellishment techniques used in this book's projects appear throughout, and are numbered in their upper left corners. Explanations of these concepts are correspondingly numbered and are included within the text of the book. Follow these steps to cut the pieces for a Double Wedding Ring quilt accurately:

1 The *wedge* template is used to cut the four center pieces of each arc. Place the four fabrics you want to feature in your wedges on top of each other in single layers. That way, each stack of pieces you cut will be enough to assemble one arc. *Note:* If you are using print fabrics, layer the first two fabrics right sides together and layer the third and fourth fabrics right sides together. The pieces will then be in the correct positions when it is time to sew them together.

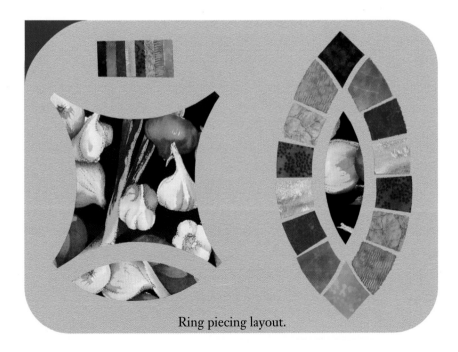

Ring piecing layout.

2 Next, you will need the *end piece* template, which is used to cut the pieces that go at each end of the arcs. *Note:* The end pieces are asymmetrical. Place the two fabrics for these pieces right sides together, so that your cut pieces will be mirror images. After you cut one pair of end pieces, take a moment to lay out four wedges with an end piece at each end to ensure that your fabrics are positioned correctly. If you discover that you cut the end pieces incorrectly, simply flip the fabrics over and cut from the other side.

3 The *corner squares* are the pointed pieces at the ends of the completed melons where the rings intersect. You will need to sew a corner square at each end of only half of the total number of arcs you make. Usually, Double Wedding Ring quilts feature two different fabrics in the corner squares, both of which are used in each arc. Doublefold the two fabrics for your corner squares because these pieces are symmetrical. Then place the corner square template on the fabric so that the right-angled edges lie along the straight of grain. Rotary cut the number of corner squares you need for your quilt.

4 To cut the *background* pieces, you'll need the templates for the large background piece and the melon shape. Prepare the fabric for cutting these pieces by folding it in half, matching the selvages. Then bring the selvages up to the center fold, creating four layers of fabric. There is very little fabric waste when you lay the templates as closely together as possible. Place the large background template on top of the fabric, sliding it toward the double fold, so that there is just enough room to cut a stack of melons next to the selvage edges. Also cut another stack of melons next to the raw edges of the fabric, as shown.

Then position the large background template and cut out a stack of large background pieces. Cut another stack of melons to the right of the large background pieces and then move the template over and cut another stack of large background pieces. Finally, cut more melons from the areas at the double fold of the fabric.

Using a Design Wall A design wall is essential for laying out many of the projects in this book. Taking the pieces of a wallhanging from a flat table and displaying them on a vertical surface allows you to see your work in the same way that viewers will see your finished quilt. If it seems impossible to find enough space to set up a vertical design wall, a bit of creativity may solve the problem. A 4' x 8' sheet of rigid foam insulation is ideal for making a design wall that will accommodate all of the projects in the book, since they are less than 48" wide. You can either fasten the sheet to a wall with washers and screws, or simply lean it

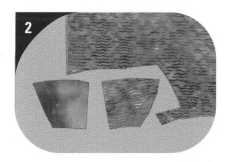

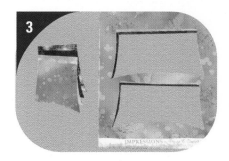

against a wall and store it elsewhere when you need to use the space for something else. You can also cut the sheet in half and add a hinge made of duct tape, so it will take less space to store. Another option is a large piece of foam core board which is both lightweight and easy to store. Cover it with felt, fleece, or flannel, so that the pieces of your quilt will stick to the surface without pins. Finally, for the ultimate in portable design walls, you can simply tape a piece of thin batting or flannel to a door while you are designing, and remove it when you finish. This type of design wall will even allow you to take your designs to a guild or group meeting for input from friends.

Sewing Equipment

Machine piecing a Double Wedding Ring quilt does not require a fancy sewing machine or special presser foot. However, if you have a single-hole throat plate, be sure to use it. A wide-hole zigzag throat plate allows the needle to push tiny pieces of fabric down the hole and under the needle, while a single-hole throat plate keeps the raw edges flat and moving smoothly under the presser foot. It is also an advantage to use the narrowest presser foot you have for your machine, so you can see the edges of the pieces as you stitch. A purchased ¼" patchwork foot works well, but be aware that you will want to sew a scant ¼" and that the edges of the pieces should not show along the side of this type of presser foot as you stitch.

Machine Settings

Set your sewing machine's stitch length at 10–12 stitches per inch. If you use a longer stitch length than this, the seams will unravel as you work with the tiny pieces of a Double Wedding Ring quilt. Also, the tension on your machine should be even, so the stitches are firm and secure on both sides of your work.

Thread

Use high quality cotton thread for machine piecing. Inexpensive polyester thread can cause breaking and melting of the seams (as I have learned through first-hand experience). Choose a neutral color thread that matches the value (meaning the lightness or darkness) of the majority of the fabrics in your quilt. I use black, gray, or natural thread for all of my machine piecing.

To machine appliqué Double Wedding Rings in place onto the border fabric, use nylon monofilament thread on top of your machine, and embroidery-weight cotton thread in the bobbin. The top tension may need to be loosened slightly to prevent the bobbin thread from showing on the top.

When it comes to thread for machine quilting, almost anything goes, especially since wallhangings do not get handled or washed often. There are many beautiful rayon threads now available that add a subtle sheen to a quilt and are easy to use. Metallics vary in regard to how easy they are to use, but if you use a #16 Jeans needle, these beautiful threads can add a wonderful sparkle and secondary design element. Use embroidery-weight cotton or polyester thread in the bobbin with decorative thread.

Accurate Seam Allowances

Sewing an accurate ¼" seam allowance has never been more important than it is in curved piecing. The curved arcs in the Double Wedding Ring pattern contain multiple seams that must be accurately pieced so that you can attach the pieced arcs to the large background pieces properly.

Take a few minutes to do a test that could save you many frustrating hours of ripping out stitches. Sew all of the pieces for one arc together, press the pieced arc, and compare it to an acrylic template for a single-fabric arc. Your pieced arc should match the template within an eighth of an inch. If you need to make adjustments to the width of your seam allowance, it is best to do that before assembling any more rings for your quilt. After your test arc is successfully completed, place your stacks of wedge pairs next to your sewing machine and follow these steps to assemble the rings of your quilt.

Piecing the Melon Units

5 Pick up the top pair of wedges (fabrics 1 and 2, which are already right sides together) from the stack. Holding the threads of your sewing machine taut as you begin, sew these two wedges together, with the narrower ends of the wedges going into the sewing machine first, and starting as close to the raw edges as possible. Without breaking the thread, pick up the second pair of wedges (fabrics 3 and 4, which are already right sides together) and sew them together in the same way. Continue chain-piecing the wedge pairs together, making sure that the same two colors alter-

nate each time. After all the pairs are sewn together, cut the threads between them.

6 Sew together the two pairs of wedges that make up an arc. Continue in the same manner until all the wedge pairs are joined. Add the end pieces to both ends of each of the four-wedge units. Make sure to keep the colors in the same place on each arc, unless otherwise specified in the project instructions.

7 Lay a pieced arc wrong side up on an ironing board so that the curve looks like a frown. Press the seam allowances lightly, working from right to left, as shown. Then turn the pieced arc over to look like a smile, and press the seam allowances from right to left again to smooth out any pleats or wrinkles. Use a very light motion when pressing, so the arcs do not stretch out of shape.

8 Divide the pieced arcs in half, creating two equal stacks. Sew a corner square to each end of all the arcs in one stack, as shown (unless otherwise specified in the project instructions). Match the corner squares to the end pieces at the seam line and align the edges of the pieces ½" at a time, with the corner square on top.

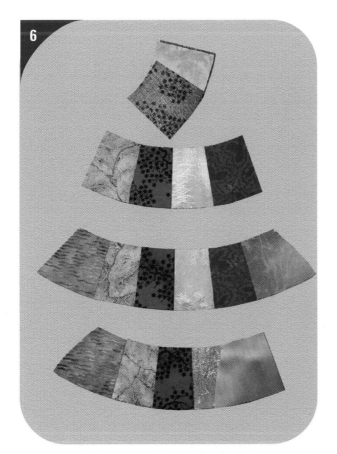

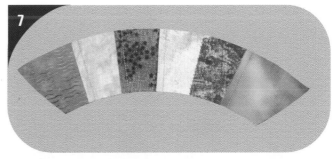

Be sure to position the colors of the corner squares the same way in each arc. Press the seam allowances of the corner squares toward the center of the arcs, as shown.

9 To sew the arcs to the melons, finger crease a center line across the width of each melon. Place an arc without corner squares on top of the melon, right sides together. Match your finger creased fold line on the melon to the center seam of the pieced arc, and pin the pieces together at this point. Pin the ends of the arc to the points of the melon, matching them at the seam line. Sew from raw edge to raw edge, with the pieced arc on top. Chain-piece all the melons and arcs in the same manner, and cut them apart. Finger press the seam allowances toward the melons.

10 Sew the remaining arcs with corner squares to the other sides of the melons. Begin by matching and pinning the center points, as before; then match the seam line between the corner squares and end pieces to the seam line you just sewed, as shown. Finally, pin the corner squares to the ends of the first pieced arcs, matching at the seam line. Sew all of the remaining arcs to the melons in the same manner.

11 Press the seam allowances toward the melons. After pressing, the melon units should lie flat, with the seams meeting perfectly at the point of the melon shape, as shown.

Joining the Rings Lay the pieced melon units and the large background pieces on a design wall in the arrangement specified in the project instructions. Then follow these steps to join the rings together.

12 To sew the melon units to the large background pieces, begin by finger creasing the center points on the four curved edges on a large background piece. Match and pin the center seam of a pieced arc in a melon unit to a center point on the large background piece. Place another pin ¼" in from the point of the large background piece; then insert the pin into the seam between the end piece and corner square of the pieced arc underneath. Pinch the fabrics together on the pin and then anchor the pin securely in the fabrics, as shown. Repeat this process at the other point of the large background piece. *Note:* The corner squares will be left hanging free. Sew this seam with the large background piece on top, backstitching at both ends.

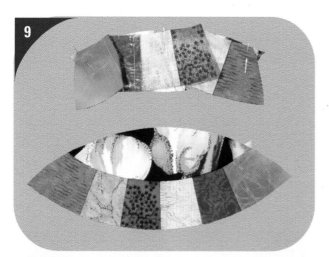

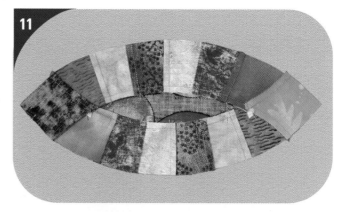

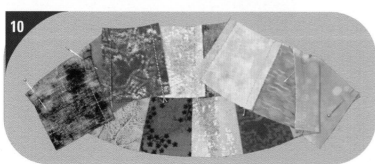

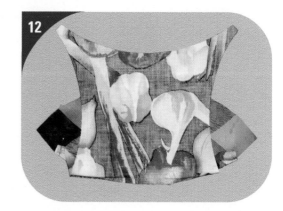

13 Continue to add complete melons to the sides of the large background pieces as needed for your project, making sure there are no two corner squares of the same fabric touching. Press the seam allowances toward the background pieces. Press as you go.

14 Sew the corner squares together to complete the rings, beginning at the raw edges and backstitching at the end of the seam, and press.

15 To join the rows of pieced rings together, start by sewing the middle ring in each row together, and work outward in both directions from there. When you have joined the rows of rings, go back and sew all of the pairs of corner squares together. When sewing the corner squares together on the outside edges, backstitch at the raw edges, so the seam allowances remain free for sewing the rings to the border. Press the seam allowances toward the background.

Machine Appliquéing the Border
After the rings are completed, there are different approaches to choose from for adding the border. If you wish to keep the edges of your quilt curved (which is especially attractive on a bed quilt), no border is necessary; two of the wall quilts in this book are bound in this way. I prefer to add a border for the added design element, the more finished look, and for ease in adding a casing to display the finished quilt. You can also add more than one border to a quilt, which makes the first border more like a background than a frame. Look through the projects in this book and decide which look you prefer, and follow these steps to add borders to your Double Wedding Ring quilts:

■ For small wall quilts, it is easiest to use a large, single layer of border fabric that extends all the way under the joined rings. The 42"–45" width of quilting cotton fabric is enough to border a quilt that is three rings (or less) across. To border a quilt that features 12 rings, you will need 1⅔ yards of border fabric. Simply tape the pressed border fabric onto a table with masking tape and place the rings (with their edges basted under) on top. Pin the rings carefully in place on the border fabric (I pin every wedge and corner square), placing the pins perpendicular to the edges of the quilt.

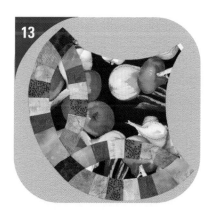

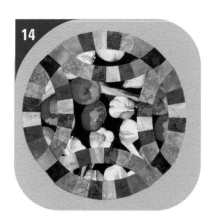

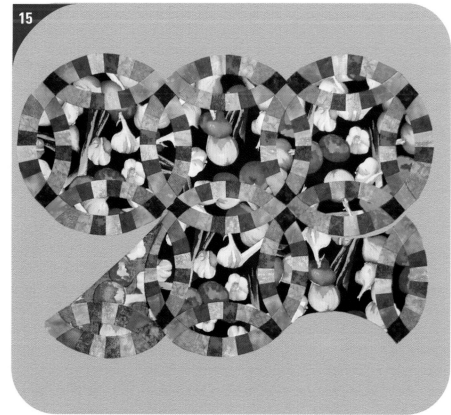

■ For machine stitching, thread your sewing machine with nylon monofilament thread on top and use a thin lingerie thread in a neutral color in the bobbin. Change to a zigzag throat plate and appliqué presser foot. Set the machine to a blind-hem stitch with a narrow width and short length. I recommend taking time to test this stitch before you begin using it to attach the rings of your quilt to the border fabric. The width of the zigzag portion of the stitch should be about ⅛" wide, and there should be a scant ¼" between the zigzags. You may need to loosen the tension on the top thread to prevent it from pulling the bobbin thread too close to the top surface, where the invisible monofilament thread could allow it to be visible.

■ Stitch around the joined rings, letting the straight stitches of the sequence fall on the border fabric and only the zigzags fall on the rings. Pivot the needle at the inner corners. After you finish stitching the rings to the border fabric, trim the borders to an equal width, using a large square acrylic ruler to square the corners. Trim out the excess border fabric from underneath the rings, leaving a ¼" seam allowance. Press the quilt top, and proceed with basting the layers for quilting, or adding more borders, if desired.

■ If you wish to avoid buying the amount of fabric required for this method of adding borders, you can use strips of border fabric instead of a single, large layer of fabric. If you choose this border option, you can either miter or butt the border corner seams, or decide to feature corner squares in your border, depending on the look you want and the amount of fabric you have available. Mitered corners require more fabric; for a twelve-ring quilt, mitered corners would require as much fabric as the method described above. For either mitered or butted corner seams, you will need to baste under the edges of the rings. Then place the border strips under the edges of the rings, extending the ends as far as necessary. The sides of the border strips should extend underneath the rings at least ¼" at the inner corners, and the centers of the border strips and the rings should match. Pin the rings and border strips together carefully, and attach each border separately, ending your stitching at the seam line between the corner squares of the rings, so that you can miter or butt the border seams later.

After stitching the borders to the rings, press the border strips in position for mitering the corner seams. Pin the border strips right sides together, and machine or hand-stitch the mitered border seams.

Machine Quilting All of the quilts in this book were machine quilted. For more information on machine quilting, check your local quilt shop for books that feature instructions on machine-guided or free-motion quilting. Or consider taking a class or workshops at a quilt shop or guild, where you can benefit from having an expert machine quilter to guide you as you learn these techniques.

Attaching the Binding For a medium-to-large wall quilt with straight edges, I recommend using a double-fold French binding. I cut my binding strips 2½" wide. For small quilts, I cut 2"-wide binding strips. In both cases, I recommend using a ¼" seam allowance. The narrower binding strips will produce a slightly narrower finished binding width which is appropriate for small wall quilts.

A few of the quilts in this book are bound with bias binding because the edges of the quilts are not straight. In these cases, instructions for adding bias binding are provided in the project.

Adding a Casing To make a casing for displaying a straight-edged wall quilt, start with a 9" x 42" strip of fabric. Trim the strip to the width of the quilt and hem under 1" at the short ends. Fold the strip in half lengthwise, wrong sides together. Pin and baste the raw edges to the top of the quilt backing, before you stitch the binding to the backing fabric. Hand sew the bottom fold of the casing to the backing; then sew the binding in place, enclosing the top edge of the casing.

For a wall quilt with curved edges, cut a 9" x 42" strip of fabric and trim it to fit the back of the quilt, just inside the indented areas along the edges. Hem the short ends and sew the raw edges together with the right sides of the fabric together. Then turn the tube right side out and press it, positioning the seam along the center on one side. Hand sew the pressed casing to the top edge of the quilt backing, stitching both of the long edges.

Home on the Prairie

Here is your chance to play! Use the Double Wedding Ring pattern as the background for an appliquéd figure. Stitch a prairie woman heading for home, as shown in this quilt, make your figure a bride with a sheer fabric veil loosely tacked over her head, or a dancer in costume. Let your imagination have free rein and create something unique and fun.

Technique: Appliquéd overlays

Finished size: 43" x 54"

Double Wedding Ring Quilts: Coming Full Circle – Susan L. Stein

Fabrics and Supplies

⅓ yard each of four print fabrics for wedges

⅓ yard each of two fabrics for end pieces

¼ yard each, of two fabrics for corner squares

1 yard for background pieces and melons

12" square for blouse, ½ yard for skirt

2¾ yards for backing

1⅔ yards for border

½ yard for binding

Scraps for hair, neck, cabin, window, and door

18" wide roll of tracing paper

Masking tape, glue stick, straight pins

Black fine-line permanent marker

Nylon monofilament thread

Cut

62 *wedges* each from four ⅓ yard pieces of fabric

62 *end pieces* each from two ⅓ yard pieces of fabric

31 *corner squares* each from two ¼ yard pieces of fabric

12 *background* large pieces and 31 *melons*

Piecing the Rings

■ Sew 31 melon units, referring to the photos on pages 11-13, and "Piecing the Melon Units" on page 11, and press.

■ Assemble the 12 rings, referring to "Joining the Rings Together" on page 12. Lay the elements of each row out next to your sewing machine to keep them in order as you sew, and take just one background piece and its pieced melons to the sewing machine at a time. Press the joined rings.

■ Turn under and baste ¼" on the edges of the rings, rounding out the corner squares at the corners of the quilt top.

Adding the Border

■ Set your sewing machine for a blind-hem stitch with a short stitch length and narrow zigzag width. Lay the rings on the border fabric and pin them in place.

■ Sew the rings to the border, referring to "Machine Appliquéing the Border" on page 13. Trim away the border fabric underneath the joined rings, leaving a ¼" seam allowance.

■ Trim the outer edges of the border fabric so they are equal in width on all sides of the quilt top. Press the completed quilt top. *Note:* Save the border fabric you trim out from behind the rings, and use it as part of the binding for the quilt, or for piecing a future Double Wedding Ring quilt.

Adding the Appliqué Overlays

■ Enlarge the appliqué pattern on page 18 to 17" x 41". To do this, lay a piece of tracing paper on top of a 1"-gridded cutting mat, and tape it in place. With a black fine-line permanent marker, draw a line across the paper every 4" for guidelines. The ¼" squares on the pattern page correspond to the 1" squares showing through your tracing paper. Transfer the lines of the design to the tracing paper, square by square. After you have enlarged the design, trace it onto another piece of tracing paper, so you have one drawing to keep and one to cut apart. *Note:* You can also draw your own freehand interpretation of the appliqué figure on page 18.

■ Cut out the skirt piece, and pin it to your skirt fabric. Cut around the pattern and remove the tracing paper.

■ Lay the blouse portion of the pattern on your blouse fabric, and cut it out; allow approximately ½" extra at the waistline so that you can tuck it under the skirt.

■ Lay the hair pattern on your hair fabric, and cut it out in the same manner.

■ Cut the neck pattern out of your neck fabric in the same manner, allowing ½" extra to tuck under at the top and bottom edges.

■ With the quilt top lying on a table, pin the uncut tracing paper pattern on top. Slide the fabric appliqué pieces for the figure underneath the tracing paper, and glue-stick them in place on the quilt top. Use the glue stick sparingly; place dots of glue only around the edges of the appliqué pieces, so trimming out the background fabric later will be easy. *Note:* Remember that the neck piece needs to lie underneath both the blouse and the hair, and the blouse needs to lie under the skirt. After you have positioned all of the appliqués on the quilt top, remove the tracing paper pattern.

■ Set your sewing machine for satin stitching, and machine appliqué around the edges of the figure, changing thread colors to match each fabric. Be sure to hold the quilt top flat and taut as you work so the satin stitching does not draw extra fabric into your stitches. *Note:* Another option is to place blank newsprint underneath the quilt top to stabilize the fabric as you satin stitch the overlays in place.

■ Satin stitch the details in the skirt, waistband, and blouse, after the figure is stitched in place, referring to the photo on page 15. Then trim the background away underneath the appliquéd areas, leaving a $\frac{1}{4}$" seam allowance.

■ Prepare the cabin: Cut out a cabin piece from a 6" scrap of light-colored fabric or muslin. Shape the roof of the cabin by folding the square in half and cutting an angle from the halfway point of the sides to the fold line.

■ Cut out a $2\frac{1}{2}$" x $1\frac{1}{4}$" door and a $1\frac{1}{2}$" x 1" window from scraps of fabric. Satin stitch the window and door to the cabin, placing blank newsprint underneath to stabilize your work. Add machine-stitched details, such as window panes, referring to the photo on page 15.

■ Satin stitch the cabin to the quilt top. Trim out the pieced rings from behind the cabin, leaving a $\frac{1}{4}$" seam allowance.

Machine Quilting

After pressing the completed quilt top, layer the backing, batting, and quilt top. Baste the layers together with thread or rust-proof safety pins.

■ Quilt in the seam lines of the rings and around the outlines and detail stitching of the figure and the cabin.

■ Referring to the photo, quilt the detail lines on the hair.

16 Use gently waving quilting lines to add a feeling of movement to the hair.

■ Trace the sunflower quilting design from page 18 onto a separate piece of tracing paper for each large

background area where you wish to quilt this design. Pin these tracing paper patterns to the large background areas and machine quilt the sunflower designs through the paper. After you finish quilting, gently remove the paper pattern from each background area.

■ Quilt the border areas in a free-motion pattern of interwoven lines.

Finishing

■ Cut five $2\frac{1}{2}$" x 42" binding strips, and bind the quilt, referring to "Attaching the Binding" on page 14.

■ Add a casing to the top edge of the back side of the quilt, referring to "Adding a Casing" on page 14.

For the details in the figure I used satin-stitch appliqué which is easy and fast, but you could also choose to do hand appliqué.

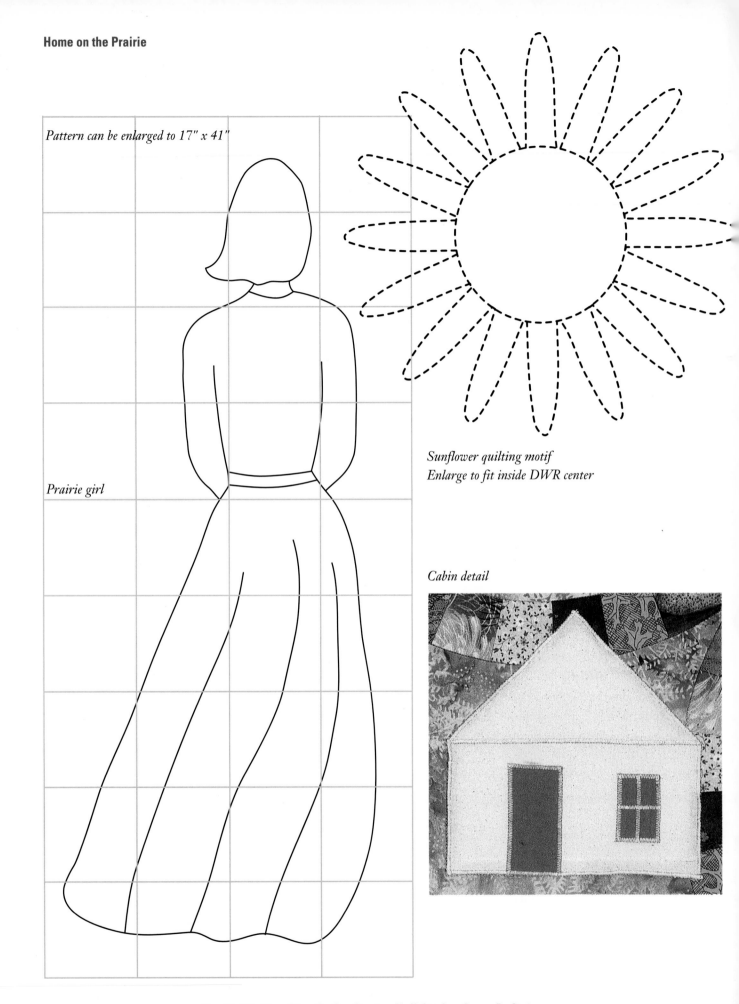

Pattern can be enlarged to 17" x 41"

Prairie girl

Sunflower quilting motif
Enlarge to fit inside DWR center

Cabin detail

Sky Trails

Start with a wonderful piece of background fabric and create a wallhanging with sparkle and eye-catching appeal. Subtle color gradations in the pieced rings carry the eye around the surface of the quilt, and the silk ribbon and beads add texture and light. The beading also acts as the quilting because the stitching goes through all three layers of the quilt. Bias binding around the rings, rather than a border, lends an airy, fluid quality to the finished quilt.

Technique: Beaded silk ribbon   Finished size: 47" x 36"

Fabrics and Supplies*

1 fat quarter (or 19" square) each of eight hand-dye fabrics, or ⅓ yd. each of eight solid fabrics for pieced arcs

1 yard of "sky" fabric for background pieces and melons

½ yard of fabric for binding

Assortment of small glass beads

12 yards of ⅛"-wide silk ribbon in assorted colors

Cotton quilting thread for beading

Size #10 Sharp needles for beading

*See Resources, pages 94-95

Cut

62 *wedge* pieces each from four colors of hand-dyed fabric (or fabrics #3–#6 from fat quarters)

62 *end* pieces each from two colors (or fabrics #2 and #7 from fat quarters)

31 *corner squares* each from the two fabrics for corner squares (or fabrics #1 and #8 from fat quarters)

12 *background* large pieces, 31 *melons* from the "sky" fabric

Piecing the Rings

■ Sew 31 melon units, referring to the instructions and photos for "Piecing the Melon Units" on page 11, press.

■ Assemble the 12 rings, see "Joining the Rings" on page 12. If you are using a directional background fabric such as the fabric in the quilt shown on page 19, it is helpful to place the background pieces on a design wall and place a pin near the tops of the large pieces so it is easy to keep them properly oriented as you sew the rings together. Press the joined rings.

■ Turn under and baste ¼" on the edges of the rings, rounding out the corner squares on the corners of the quilt top. *Note:* This quilt features hand-painted "sky" fabrics. See Resources, page 92-93, Books and Fabrics, for the exact fabric used in this quilt and for information on a book that will tempt you to try painting your own fabric.

Machine Quilting

■ Press the completed quilt top. Use thin batting to avoid making large "dents" in the quilt when you do the beading. Layer the backing, batting, and quilt top, and baste the layers together with thread or rust-proof safety pins. Machine quilt in the seam lines of the rings.

Adding the Silk Ribbon and Beads

■ Lay a 1- to 2-yard length of the ribbon on the quilt top. The ends of the ribbon can extend beyond the edge of the quilt top, or stop anywhere you wish within the rings.

■ Thread a size #10 Sharp with thread for beading and make a knot in the end. Slide the needle into a seam allowance to bury the knot in the batting. Bring the needle out of the quilt top, catching one end of the ribbon. Make a couple of quilting stitches through all of the layers (including the ribbon), and add a bead to the next stitch. Continue to stitch the ribbon to the quilt in this manner, twisting and curving it as you go, and adding a bead every two or three stitches. When your thread gets short, pull the needle to the back side of the quilt. Then point the needle toward the quilt, wrap the thread around the needle several times (like a French

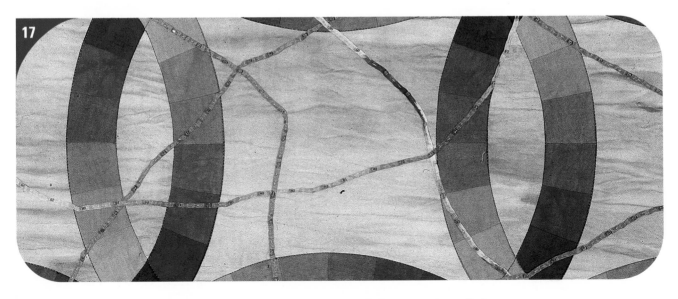

knot), and stick the needle through the fabric into the batting layer. Pull the needle out of the backing fabric ½" away, and pull on the thread while scraping the knot with your fingernail to ease the knot under the surface of the fabric into the batting.

■ Hang the quilt on the design wall, after you finish stitching the first length of ribbon in place to see where you want to place the next length of ribbon. Stitch and bead the second length of ribbon in the same manner as the first. When you feel that you have embellished the surface of the quilt consistently, you're done!

17 Ribbons sewn to the quilt with seed beads act as the quilting in the background areas.

Finishing

■ Lay the half-yard length of binding fabric wrong side up in a single layer on a cutting table. With a yardstick and pencil, draw a line diagonally on the fabric. Continue drawing parallel lines 2" apart in each direction from the first, until you have drawn five bias strips. Using scissors, cut on the pencil lines. *Note:* A 2" x 60" metal ruler is great for rotary cutting long bias binding strips. Look for this type of ruler at art supply stores. Put a few self-adhesive sandpaper dots on the back so it won't slip as you move the rotary cutter along the side.

■ Connect the bias strips end to end by laying one strip at right angles on top of another strip with the right sides together. Sew the strips together diagonally, starting and ending where the strips cross each other at the edges. Trim away the excess fabric, leaving a ¼" seam allowance. Press these seams open.

■ Press the binding in half, with the wrong sides together. Starting on a curved edge of the quilt top, turn under the end of the binding strip at an angle and sew it onto the quilt through all the layers, matching the edges. Do not stretch the binding strip as you sew, or it will pull the edges of the rings up and the finished quilt will not lie flat. When you reach the inner corners, lower the needle at the seam intersections and pivot, using a stiletto or a seam ripper to pull the binding around to the next curved edge. At the four outer curves, take less seam allowance on the corner squares to round out the curves. When you reach the starting point, overlap the turned-under end ½" and cut off the remaining portion of the binding.

■ Trim away the excess batting and backing fabric even with the edges of the rings. Clip into the inside corners. Turn the binding to the back side of the quilt and hand-stitch it just over the sewing line, using a blind stitch. At the inner corners, pleat the excess binding to create a miter, as shown here, and take a couple of extra stitches to hold it securely in place.

18 Miters are folded in as the binding is sewn in place on the back side of the quilt.

■ To display the quilt, add a casing to the top edge of the backing fabric, referring to "Adding a Casing" on page 14.

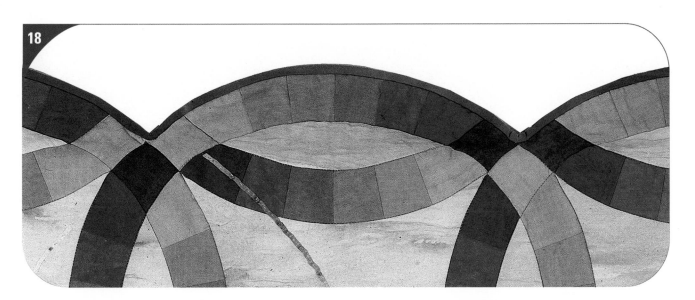

Reflections on a Line

This quilt shows the play of light and dark in several ways. The dark and murky background fabric called for the addition of light-catching craft foil that echoes the lines of an overdyed drapery print. The hand-dyed fabrics in the pieced arcs create a blend that goes from a rose color to black. The black piping around the rings separates them effectively from the lighter border fabric which might otherwise have faded into the ring colors. Finally, metallic quilting thread adds another reflective element and brings the quilt to life, especially when viewed at close range.

Technique: Adding piping and craft foil

Finished size: 42" square

Double Wedding Ring Quilts: Coming Full Circle – Susan L. Stein

Fabrics and Supplies*

1 fat quarter (or 19" square) each of eight hand-dyed fabrics, or ⅓ yd. each of eight solid fabrics for pieced arcs

1 yard of fabric for background pieces and melons

1⅓ yards of fabric or 42" square of fabric for border

½ yard of fabric for binding

Two packages (5 yds.) of piping

One 8"x10" sheet craft foil

Iron-on double-stick fusible web

Walking or even-feed foot for adding piping and machine-guided quilting

Darning foot for free-motion quilting

*See Resources, pages 94-95

Cut

48 *wedges* each from four colors (fabrics #3–#6 from a hand-dyed bundle)

48 *end* pieces each from two colors (fabrics #2 and #7 from a hand-dyed bundle)

24 *corner squares* each from two colors (fabrics #1 and #8 from a hand-dyed bundle)

9 *background* large pieces and 24 melons

Four 5" x 44" strips or a 42" square of fabric for border

Piecing the Rings

■ Sew 24 melon units, referring to "Piecing the Melon Units" on page 11 and the photos on pages 11-13, and press.

■ Assemble the 9 rings, referring to "Joining the Rings" on page 12. Lay the elements of each row on a design wall or next to your sewing machine to keep them in order as you sew. Take just one background

piece and its pieced melons to the sewing machine at a time. Press the joined rings.

■ Turn under and baste a ¼" seam allowance around the edges of the rings to prepare for adding the border strips; place the piping next to the fold, and include it in the basting as you stitch. Start and end the piping at inside corners and do a few extra basting stitches at the remaining inside corners to hold the piping securely in place. Take special care to round out the outer curves along the corner squares, by reducing the seam allowance width to ⅛" in these areas.

Adding the Border Strips

■ Position the 4 border strips underneath the rings, one at a time, making sure there is a ¼" seam allowance lying underneath the inner corners, and matching the center of the strips to the center of the rings on each side of the quilt. Pin the border strips in place.

■ Set your sewing machine for blind-hem appliqué with a short stitch length and narrow stitch width. Machine appliqué the rings to the border strips one at a time, being careful to sew through the seam allowance of the piping but not the actual piping itself. Your machine's normal appliqué foot should be able to ride on top of the piping without interference.

19 Use black commercial piping to highlight the colors and shapes of the rings.

■ Miter the border corner seams by folding one border strip over the adjacent border strip at a 45-degree

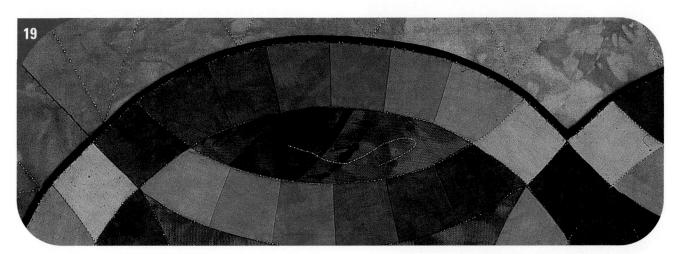

angle and using blind-hem appliqué to stitch the fold in place. Trim the mitered seam allowances to ¼".

Adding Foil Details

■ Place the quilt top on a design wall. Cut pieces of fusible web in shapes that coordinate with the pattern in your background fabric. Remove the backing paper from one side of the fusible web, and position the web shape on the fabric wherever you would like to position the foil; leave the top layer of paper over the web. Continue adding pieces of web, standing back to check placements from a distance. When you are happy with the placements of the shapes, press them lightly to tack the web to the fabric. *Note:* Read through the following step and do a test sample with some scrap fabrics before adding foil to your quilt top.

■ Carefully place the quilt top on an ironing board. Remove the backing paper from one of the web shapes. Place a sheet of foil, color side up, over the cut web shape, and use the edge of a dry iron to rub over the sheet of foil, transferring the foil to the web. Allow the foil to cool and carefully peel the cellophane away from the foil. If the web is not covered completely, repeat this process with another spot on the sheet of foil.

20 Silver metallic foil and quilting thread add light and dynamic detail to this dark color scheme.

■ Remove the backing paper from another shape and add foil to your next design. Be careful to clean up any stray particles of web before applying the iron to a new foil shape. (See Resources, page 92, Books, for a reference on foiling.)

Machine Quilting

■ Press the completed quilt top, using a non-stick press cloth to avoid damaging the areas with foil.

■ Layer the backing, batting, and quilt top, and baste the layers together with thread or rust-proof safety pins.

■ Using a walking or even-feed foot on your sewing machine, *quilt in the seam lines of the rings*, using metallic thread to match the foil. The walking or even-feed foot should ride on top of the piping so that you can quilt between it and the edges of the rings.

■ Change to a darning foot, and lower or cover the feed dogs on your sewing machine. *Free-motion quilt lines* that compliment the foil shapes in the large background areas.

■ On the borders, quilt a large zigzag that bounces from the piping to the binding, using the walking or even-feed foot. Take care to make the corners neat and consistent in pattern.

Finishing

■ Cut five 2½" x 42" binding strips, and bind the quilt, referring to "Attaching the Binding" on page 14.

■ Add a casing to the top edge of the back side of the quilt, referring to "Adding a Casing" on page 14.

Afterglow

Vintage hand-dyed kimono silk was used for the background and melons of this quilt. The small crazy-quilt shapes are fused to interfacing to hold them in place which made it easy to add fancy stitching by machine. Choose a pretty, decorative thread to cover the edges of the pieces and solid red arcs that stand out yet complement the background areas.

Technique: Crazy quilting

Finished size: 41" x 30"

Fabrics and Supplies*

⅞ yard of solid fabric for one-piece arcs

¼ yard each of two fabrics for corner squares

Small pieces of assorted fabrics for background pieces and melons

⅞ yard of fabric for border

⅓ yard of fabric for binding

¾ yard of fusible, woven-cotton interfacing

Rayon thread

Glue stick

Walking or even-feed foot for machine-guided quilting

Darning foot for free-motion quilting

*See Resources, pages 94-95

Cut

34 *one-piece arcs* from the solid fabric

17 *corner squares* each from the two fabrics for corner squares

6 *background* large pieces from the woven interfacing, adding ¼" extra around all of the edges as you cut

17 *melons* from the assorted fabrics

Piecing the Rings

■ Sew a corner square in each color to the ends of half of the one-piece arcs.

■ Sew an arc with corner pieces and an arc without corner pieces to each of the 17 melons, and press.

■ Lay an interfacing background piece on an ironing board with the adhesive side facing up. Cut enough small pieces of scrap fabrics to cover the interfacing shape, overlapping the edges of the pieces slightly. Fuse the pieces to the interfacing, following the manufacturer's instructions. Repeat the same process to cover each of the nine interfacing background pieces with randomly shaped pieces. *Note:* Use a glue stick to hold down any overlapping edges that did not bond to the interfacing.

■ Set your sewing machine to a short stitch length and a medium-to-wide stitch width. Select a fancy satin stitch you like from the options available on your machine; look for one that will cover the edges of the crazy quilt pieces. Thread your machine with a decorative thread that coordinates with your fabrics and sew along all of the raw edges of the fused shapes, changing stitch patterns as you wish. Press the completed background pieces and trim them to the correct size.

■ Arrange the background pieces on a design wall, balancing the colors, and add the melon units between them. When you are happy with your arrangement, sew the six rings together, and press.

■ Turn under and baste a ¼" seam allowance on the edges of the joined rings.

Adding the Border

■ Set your sewing machine for a blind-hem stitch with a short stitch length and narrow zigzag width. Lay the rings on the border fabric and pin them in place securely.

■ Sew the rings to the border, referring to "Machine Appliquéing the Border" on page 13. Trim away the border fabric underneath the joined rings, leaving a ¼" seam allowance.

■ Trim the outer edges of the border fabric so they are equal in width on all sides of the quilt top. Press the completed quilt top.

Machine Quilting

■ Press the completed quilt top.

■ Layer backing, batting, and quilt top, and baste the layers together with thread or rust-proof safety pins.

■ Using a walking or even-feed foot on your sewing machine, quilt in the seam lines of the rings. Using thread that matches the satin stitching, quilt along the lines of fancy stitching on the background pieces.

21 The quilting is done in the same rayon thread as the decorative satin stitching around the appliqué.

■ Change to a darning foot, and lower or cover the feed dogs on your sewing machine. Free-motion quilt the border by stitching leaves or loops at the corner squares.

22 The border is quilted with feathers at the corner squares.

Finishing

■ Cut four 2½" x 42" binding strips, and bind the quilt, referring to "Attaching the Binding" on page 14.

■ Add a casing to the top edge of the back side of the quilt, referring to "Adding a Casing" on page 14.

Lilianna

You can master fabric painting easily in a day, and it opens up all kinds of possibilities for painting appliqués and background fabrics. The water and salt do all the work of making patterns on the fabric, and all you have to do is quickly brush on some color to start the process. The raw edges of the silk petals and leaves are burned to keep them from raveling and add a touch of gray to the brightness of the color scheme.

Techniques: Fabric painting and burned-silk appliqué

Finished size: 37" square

Double Wedding Ring Quilts: Coming Full Circle – Susan L. Stein

Fabrics and Supplies*

Red, yellow, blue, magenta, turquoise, and black fabric paints that leave fabric soft after painting

4 yds. of 10–12 mm (40"–45"-wide) white silk twill or china silk fabric for painting

7 yards of 22"-wide knit or woven cotton fusible interfacing

Silk salt or other coarse salt

Sponge brush

Plastic garbage bags

Spray bottle filled with water

Small plastic cups for mixing paint

Glue stick

Decorative thread or nylon monofilament thread

Walking or even-feed foot for machine-guided quilting

Darning foot for free-motion quilting

*See Resources, pages 94-95

Painting the Silk Fabric

Note: The instructions that follow are for painting individual pieces of silk fabric with one color to be used in piecing the quilt top. Be sure to work in a well-ventilated area to avoid inhaling paint fumes.

■ Tear five ½-yard pieces from the silk yardage. Tear these pieces in half to make 10 fat quarters, each 18" x 22".

■ Lay the first fat quarter on a garbage bag that is slightly larger than the fabric. Spray the fabric with water until it is very damp.

■ Pour a color of paint into a cup and add water, mixing with a sponge brush until the paint drips quickly off the brush. Brush the paint over the surface of the wet fabric. If the paint is too thick in some spots, use a spray bottle filled with water to mist the fabric; then smooth the paint out with the sponge brush until the fabric is covered evenly with color. *Note:* Try mixing your own colors. You can't create an ugly color using only primary colors (red, yellow, and blue), unless you mix red with green, yellow with purple, or blue with orange, which are opposite each other on the color wheel and will produce brownish-green.

■ Sprinkle salt sparingly over the surface and move the plastic garbage bag and silk to a safe place for drying. Brush strokes aren't important, as long as you cover the entire surface of the silk with paint. It will run and be pushed around by the salt to create interesting patterns as it dries. Even the folds and wrinkles in the plastic underneath will make interesting patterns on the silk.

Note: Sometimes adding a few drops of one color to a second color is all you need to do to create an exciting color. You can also mix half-and-half colors for interesting variations. Try adding a little black to some colors to darken them. Or leave paint on the sponge brush and go directly to the next paint color and a new piece of fabric to see interesting colors emerge.

■ Paint each of the remaining nine pieces of silk a different color, so you can use them for the pieced arcs, flowers, and leaves. If the colors you paint do not include a good color for leaves, tear one more half-yard piece of silk fabric into two fat quarters; paint one of these fat quarters green for leaves and the other in a flower color you like.

■ After the paint dries thoroughly, press the silk fabric pieces for 30 seconds with a hot iron, moving the iron constantly to avoid scorching the fabric. Throw the pieces in the washer with a mild soap to remove the salt and soften the fabric. Dry the silk pieces until slightly damp and then press them.

■ Rinse, dry, and press the remaining white silk fabric to preshrink it and prevent possible water marks from occurring later.

Cut

Note: Preshrink the interfacing to improve its performance; soak it for a few minutes in warm water and dry it on low heat.

■ Tear an 18" strip from the large, unpainted piece of silk fabric, and set it aside for the binding. Also set aside the extra pieces of silk fabric you painted for the leaves and flowers.

■ Fuse the 10 painted fat quarters and the remaining piece of unpainted silk fabric to the interfacing to stabilize the silk and make it easier to work with. Cut:

48 *wedges* each from four colors of the painted silk
48 *end pieces* each from two colors of the painted silk
24 *corner squares* each from two colors of the painted silk
9 *background* large pieces and 24 *melons* from the interfaced white silk

Piecing the Rings

■ Sew 24 melon units, referring to the photos on pages 11-13 and "Piecing the Melon Units" on page 11, and press.

■ Assemble the 9 rings, referring to "Joining the Rings" on page 12. Lay the elements of each row on a design wall or next to your sewing machine to keep them in order as you sew. Take just one background piece and its pieced melons to the sewing machine at a time. Press the joined rings.

Machine Quilting

■ Layer the backing, batting, and quilt top, and baste the layers together with thread or rust-proof safety pins.

■ Using a walking or even-feed foot on your sewing machine, quilt in the seam lines of the rings. You can either bind the quilt at this point or wait until you finish appliquéing the leaves and flowers in place.

Burning the Flower Petals and Leaves

■ Peel the interfacing away from the leftover silk fabric, and free-form cut petals and leaves out of the fabrics you painted for the pieced arcs and the extra fabrics you painted for the leaves and flowers. Referring to the photo on page 31 for guidance on size and shape, cut approximately five to six flower petals and two to four leaves for each large background area. Make these shapes very simple and be sure to cut them a little bit larger than you want the finished pieces to be because they will be smaller after the edges are burned. *Note*: For the following steps, be sure to work in a ventilated area because the burning silk will have an odor. Also, make sure that you place a container of

water nearby, so you can immediately put out flames from any silk that starts to burn too fast or gets wax on it. If an edge starts to burn, blow it out carefully, rather than shaking the fabric, which could spread hot particles over your work area and cause injury.

■ Using a pair of tweezers, hold the petals and leaves to the side of a candle flame, inserting them into the flame with quick in-and-out motions. This will seal the edges and keep them from raveling, and it will add an attractive gray edge to the brightly colored silk. You have plenty of painted silk to play with, so don't be afraid to experiment. After you have burned the petals and leaves, place them on paper towels and rub the edges firmly, moving away from the edge to remove all of the soot and the hard, crumbly bits of silk. *Note*: Avoid holding silk leaves or petals at the top of a candle flame, which will discolor the fabric with soot.

Adding the Petals and Leaves

■ Using a glue stick, very lightly glue the petals and leaves onto the large background areas, referring to the photo on page 28 for placement ideas or create your own original flowers. Scatter some additional petals and leaves randomly around the quilt top.

■ Change to a darning foot and lower the feed dogs on your sewing machine. Free-motion quilt ⅛" in from the edges of the petals and leaves. Stitch veins into the leaves, too, if you wish. I used rayon thread that coordinated with the colors of the painted silk fabric in my quilt. You could also use invisible nylon monofilament thread. Begin and end these lines of free-motion quilting with several tiny stitches, clipping the thread close to the surface of the fabric after you finish. Brush away any burned particles that may have come off the edges of the flower petals and leaves.

23 The leaves and petals are stitched ⅛" in from the edges, securing them in place and quilting the layers of the quilt at the same time.

Finishing

■ Lay the reserved white silk binding fabric in a single layer on a cutting table. With a yardstick and pencil, draw a line diagonally from corner to corner on the fabric. Continue drawing parallel lines 2" apart in each direction from the original line, until you have drawn four bias strips. Cut on the pencil lines with scissors, or if you have a 2" x 48" metal ruler, you can use it to cut the strips with a rotary cutter.

■ Join the bias strips end to end by laying one strip at right angles on top of another strip, right sides together. Sew the strips together with a diagonal seam, starting and ending where the strips cross each other at the edges. Trim away the excess fabric, leaving a ¼" seam allowance. Press this seam open. Join the remaining binding strips together in the same manner.

■ Press the binding in half with the wrong sides together. Starting on a curve, turn under the end of the binding strip at an angle and sew it onto the quilt through all layers, matching the edges. Do not stretch the binding as you sew or it will pull the edges of the

rings up and the finished quilt will not lie flat. At the inner corners, lower the needle at the seam intersections and pivot, using a seam ripper or stiletto to pull the binding around to the next curve. When you reach the four outer curves, take a narrower seam allowance to round out the curves. When you reach the starting point, overlap the turned-under end ½" and cut off the remaining portion of the binding.

■ Trim the excess batting and backing fabric even with the edges of the rings. Clip into the inside corners. Turn the binding to the back side of the quilt and hand sew it just over the sewing line. At the inner corners, pleat the excess binding to create a miter and take a couple of extra stitches to hold it in place.

■ Add a casing to the top edge on the back of the quilt, just under the inner corners of the rings, referring to "Adding a Casing" on page 14.

Double Wedding Ring Quilts: Coming Full Circle – Susan L. Stein

Flower Crossings

Make this simple wall quilt bloom with colors that cheer up a room and remind you of your favorite flower garden. Use a combination of machine-guided and free-motion quilting to add the stems and leaves to your "flowers."

Technique: Abstract pieced "flowers" and "leaves"   Finished size: 53" x 31"

Double Wedding Ring Quilts: Coming Full Circle – Susan L. Stein

Fabrics and Supplies*

⅓ yard each of two print fabrics for "flowers"

⅓ yard each of four print fabrics for "leaves"

¼ yard each of two print fabrics for "flower centers"

⅔ yard of printed-gradation fabric or other fabric that will show quilting for background pieces

1⅝ yards of fabric for border

⅜ yard of fabric for binding

Nylon monofilament thread

Variegated decorative threads for stems and leaves

#16 Jeans needle

Chalk pencil

Walking or even-feed foot for machine-guided quilting

Darning foot for free-motion quilting

*See Resources, pages 94-95

Cut

44 *wedges* each from the four leaf colors

44 *end pieces* each from two flower colors; work with the fabrics folded instead of in single layers; you will be cutting 22 pieces of each color turned one way and 22 of each color turned the other way

22 *corner squares* from each of the two flower center colors.

22 *melons* and 8 *background* large pieces from the printed-gradation fabric

Piecing the Arcs to Suggest Flowers and Leaves

■ Sew together four wedges for each of the 44 arcs.

■ Add two colors of end pieces to 22 of the arcs; be careful not to sew the same color to both ends of the same arc. The colors of the end pieces will become the colors of the "flowers."

■ Switch the positions of the colors of the end pieces as you sew them to the remaining 22 arcs. This will ensure that the colors of the "flowers" will alternate in the finished quilt top.

■ Sew the corner squares to the 22 pieced arcs from the previous step, always placing the same color corner squares next to the same color end pieces. This will ensure that the "flower" colors will go all the way around the corner square intersections in the finished quilt top.

Joining the Rings

■ Arrange the background pieces on a design wall to maintain the values of the printed-gradation fabric.

■ Add the pieced arcs on each side of the background pieces so the same colors meet at each intersection of corner squares. Step back and view your arrangement from a distance to confirm that the "flower" colors go all the way around each corner square intersection.

24 Fabrics were chosen to suggest flowers, flower centers, and leaves.

■ Sew the pieced arcs to the melons, referring to "Piecing the Melon Units" on page 11, and taking pieces as needed from the design wall to keep all of the pieces in proper order.

■ Assemble the eight rings, referring to the photo on page 13 and "Joining the Rings" on page 12, and press.

■ Turn under and baste ¼" seam allowances on the edges of the joined rings.

Adding the Border

■ Set your sewing machine for a blind-hem stitch with a short stitch length and narrow zigzag width. Lay the rings on the border fabric and pin them in place securely.

■ Sew the rings to the border, referring to "Machine Appliquéing the Border" on page 13. Trim away the border fabric underneath the joined rings, leaving a ¼" seam allowance.

■ Trim the outer edges of the border fabric so they are equal in width on all sides of the quilt top. Press the completed quilt top.

Machine Quilting

■ Baste the quilt top, batting, and backing together, referring to "Machine Quilting" on page 14.

■ Using a walking or even-feed foot on your sewing machine and decorative thread, quilt inside the seam lines of the rings.

■ Using a chalk pencil, mark diagonal "stem" lines from point to point on the background areas. Using decorative thread, machine quilt these lines using the walking or even-feed foot and a #16 Jeans needle.

■ Change to a darning foot and free-motion quilt leaves along the stitched "stems."

25 Variegated thread adds interest to the stem and leaf quilting in the background areas.

■ Free-motion quilt the border in a large stipple pattern, filling in the inner corners of the rings and the outer corners of the border.

26 Variegated thread is also used for the stipple quilting in the border.

Finishing

■ Cut five 2½" x 42" binding strips and bind the quilt, referring to "Attaching the Binding" on page 14.

■ Add a casing to the top edge of the back side of the quilt. To make a casing for displaying a straight-edged wall quilt, start with a 9" x 42" strip of fabric. Trim the strip to the width of the quilt and hem under 1" at the short ends. Fold the strip in half lengthwise, wrong sides together. Pin and baste the raw edges to the top of the quilt backing before you stitch the binding to the backing fabric. Hand sew the bottom fold of the casing to the backing; then sew the binding in place, enclosing the top edge of the casing.

Rings on Squares

Have fun choosing the fabrics for this wall quilt. Depending on the fabrics you choose, you can make the rings stand out visually or recede into the background squares. Consider creating a watercolor effect with a lot of floral prints, choose soft, gradated hand-dyed fabrics, or accentuate the checkerboard effect with a high level of contrast between colors, as I did. This is a great project for using fat quarters or scraps, and it's easy to piece and appliqué with no curved piecing or complicated cutting. Add some glitz with metallic threads and a lot of simple free-motion quilting.

Techniques: Pieced background and appliquéd rings   Finished size: 42" square

Fabrics and Supplies*

¼ yard each of six dark fabrics for background squares

¼ yard each of six light print fabrics for background squares

⅔ yard of a dark contrast-color fabric for the four corner rings

½ yard each of two bright contrast-color fabrics for the side rings

½ yard of dark fabric for the center ring

½ yard of contrast-color fabric for binding

16" square of medium-thick mat board (*Note*: This will get damp, so avoid any color that could bleed.)

Liquid starch (bottle or spray can)

Decorative threads

Craft or utility knife with sharp blade

Darning foot for free-motion quilting

*See Resources, pages 94-95

Cut

■ Layer the six dark and six light print fabrics, three at a time; cut two 3½" x 42" strips from each fabric. Cut these strips into 196 squares, each 3½" x 3½".

■ Make a ring template by drawing a 15" circle on the mat board. Draw a 12" circle inside the larger circle. Cut out the ring with a sharp craft or utility knife. *Note*: You can also ask a frame shop to cut the mat board circle for you.

■ Lay the ring template on the dark fabric for the center ring. Using scissors, cut a full ¼" seam allowance around the inner and outer edges of the template by eye.

■ Using the ring template, mark and cut 4 dark and 4 bright contrast-color rings in the same manner.

Piecing the Background

■ Sew a dark print square to a light print square. Continue adding squares, alternating the dark and light print fabrics, until you have sewn a row of 14 squares. Press the seams open to avoid bulk underneath the appliquéd rings.

■ Starting with a light print square, sew a second row of 14 squares. Press the seams open as before.

■ Sew the two rows of squares together, matching seam lines. This begins to create the checkerboard background. Press the seam open.

■ Repeat this piecing process until you have created a background square that contains 14 rows of 14 squares each. Press the pieced background square well so that it lies flat with no twisted seam allowances.

Appliquéing the Rings

■ Lay the cut dark center ring on an ironing board, wrong side up. Place the ring template on top so the ¼" seam allowances are even all the way around the inner and outer edges. Pour or spray the liquid starch into a small cup. With your finger, dab starch on the ¼" seam allowances, and use the tip of a dry iron to press them around the template until they are dry and secured in place. Clip the inside curve if necessary. When the seam allowances are completely turned under, gently peel the fabric away from the ring template.

■ Repeat this step for the eight dark and bright contrast-color rings.

■ Position the dark center ring at the center of the pieced background. To do this, place the inner edge of the ring two squares out in each direction from the center of the pieced background square. Pin the edges of the ring in place, except where the ring will intersect with other rings.

■ Position the 4 dark and 4 bright contrast-color rings around the dark center ring. Remember that the finished rings measure 15" from outer edge to outer edge and 12" from inner edge to inner edge. The pieced background squares are 3" finished, so you can use the seam lines as accurate placement guides for positioning the remaining rings. Pin both edges of each contrast-color ring in place, except where the rings will cross each other.

■ After the rings are pinned onto the pieced background, interweave them, referring to the photo on page 35. To do this, start by weaving the dark center ring over and under the surrounding contrast-color rings. *Note*: To weave one ring under another, use scissors to cut the underlying ring, and place the cut edges underneath the ring on top. After you finish weaving the dark center ring, the other rings will be easy – just use the photo on page 35 as a guide. Pin the intersections of all of the rings to the pieced background very carefully as you go.

27 The solid appliquéd rings are interwoven at the intersections.

■ With metallic or rayon thread, top stitch the edges of the rings with straight stitching or machine appliqué them with a blind-hem stitch and nylon monofilament thread.

■ Press the completed quilt top.

Machine Quilting
■ Layer the backing, batting, and quilt top, and baste the layers together with thread or rust-proof safety pins.

■ Using a darning foot and lowering or covering the feed dogs on your sewing machine, free-motion quilt

large zigzags over the edges of the rings using metallic thread. Use a size 16 Jeans needle to make it easy to stitch through all the layers of the quilt without breaking the metallic thread.

28 Large, free-motion zigzags cover the edges of the rings with highly reflective metallic thread.

■ Quilt the pieced background squares with free-motion diagonal lines.

29 Diagonal grid quilting across the background squares adds texture.

Finishing
■ Cut five 3" x 42" contrast-color binding strips to make an extra wide binding that will also function as a thin border. Bind the quilt, referring to "Attaching the Binding" on page 14.

■ Add a casing to the top edge of the back side of the quilt, referring to "Adding a Casing" on page 14.

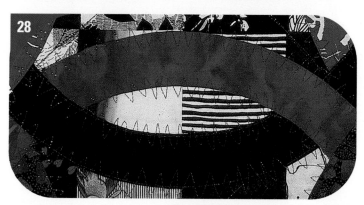

Torrid Orchid

Chenille is fun to make because you can't predict what it will look like until you either make test swatches or jump right in and make your quilt. The texture of this wallhanging is so wonderful, you may want to expand on this idea and make a warm couch throw, too. There is no batting in this project – and no binding, either! Choose a wild floral print or woven stripe for the top layer and a woven plaid, stripe, or solid for the backing. In between, you can use any cotton fabrics from your stash as long as they look similar on the right and wrong sides and vary in color.

Technique: Chenille background

Finished size: 36" square

Note: Make sure that the fabrics you select for this project are soft and will ravel easily. Avoid pima cottons, like batiks, which are closely woven. Test swatches of fabric to determine whether they will ravel well and the order in which they look best.

Fabrics and Supplies*

⅓ yard each of four fabrics for wedges

⅓ yard each of two fabrics for end pieces or choose a fat-quarter bundle of hand-dyed fabrics (19" squares) for both wedges and end pieces

¼ yard each of two fabrics for corner squares (included in fat-quarter bundles)

1¼ yards each of four different fabrics for the inside chenille layers

1¼ yards of woven plaid or other two-sided fabric for backing

#2 mechanical pencil

Walking or even-feed foot for machine-guided quilting

*See Resources, pages 94-95

Cut

48 *wedges* each from four colors (fabrics #3 through #6 from a hand-dyed bundle)

48 *end pieces* each from two colors (fabrics #2 and #7 from a hand-dyed bundle)

24 *corner squares* each of two colors (fabrics #1 and #8 from a hand-dyed bundle)

24 *melons* and 9 *background* large pieces from one of the fabrics for chenille

Piecing the Rings

■ Sew 24 melon units, referring to the photos on pages 11-13, and "Piecing the Melon Units" on page 11, and press.

■ Assemble the 9 rings, referring to "Joining the Rings" on page 12. Lay the elements of each row on a design wall or next to your sewing machine to keep them in order as you sew and take just one background piece and its pieced melons to the sewing machine at a time. Press the joined rings.

Creating the Chenille Background

■ Tape the two-sided backing fabric to a table. Lay the inner-layers of chenille fabric on top of the backing fabric and add the joined rings, right side up.

■ Using the #2 mechanical pencil, draw a line diagonally from point to point across each large background piece. Draw parallel lines ⅝" apart in each direction from these lines, ending each of these lines ¼" from the seams of the background pieces.

■ Pin or baste the joined rings, the inner layers of fabric, and the backing together securely.

■ Using a walking or even-feed foot on your sewing machine, quilt in the seam lines of the rings and ¼" from the raw edges around the quilt top.

■ Quilt along the marked pencil lines, backstitching as you end each line of stitching to hold the thread securely. Clip the threads close to the surface of the quilt.

■ Cut very carefully through the first five layers of fabric between your lines of stitching on the large background pieces, taking care to keep the backing layer of fabric intact.

■ Trim all the layers of fabric even with the raw edges of the joined rings.

■ Place the quilt in cool water in a washing machine, agitate it, and spin dry. Machine dry the quilt, removing it from the dryer periodically to shake it and trim any long threads. Remove the quilt from the dryer just before it gets completely dry.

30 Quilt diagonal lines on the large background piece, slash through several layers of colorful fabric, then wash the piece to give it a lot of texture.

■ Press the melons and rings. Trim off any long threads around the outer edges of the quilt, letting the short threads fray attractively. Lay the quilt flat or hang it on a design wall to dry completely.

31 Edges are top stitched and allowed to fray.

Note: For more great ideas on making and using chenille, see Resources, page 93, Books.

Finishing
■ Add a casing to the top edge of the back side of the quilt, referring to "Adding a Casing" on page 14.

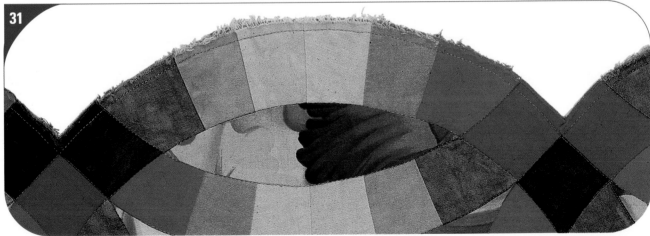

Phantom Rings

One day I cut out a background fabric and placed it on the design wall before piecing the arcs, which led me to think up yet another variation for the Double Wedding Ring pattern. Forget piecing arcs and attaching them to melons – simply choose two smashing fabrics and top stitch the background over the "ring" fabric for an instantly wonderful abstract look with none of that pesky piecing! The "ring" fabric extends beyond the appliquéd backgrounds to create the border. Add fancy quilting if you like, or let the fabrics speak for themselves as I did.

Technique: Floating background

Finished size: 40" square

Fabrics and Supplies*

1¼ yards of solid "ring" fabric

1⅜ yards of "background" print fabric (Adjust this amount if "fussy" cutting to highlight motifs in the print fabric.)

42" square of batting (I recommend a cotton/poly batting with a bit of loft.)

42" square of backing fabric

½ yard of fabric for binding

Chalk pencil

Small, stiff-bristle brush

Walking or even-feed foot for machine-guided quilting

*See Resources, pages 94-95

Cut

9 *background* large pieces and 24 *melons* including ¼" seam allowances from the "background" print fabric

One 40" square from the "ring" fabric

Creating the Floating Background

■ Fold the "ring" fabric into quarters and finger press the folds. Using the chalk pencil, draw light lines across the fabric exactly 10¾" away on both sides of each fold line.

■ Tape the 42" square of backing fabric to a table and lay the batting on top. Add the ring fabric right side up. Do not baste the layers together.

■ Finger press the center points on the sides of one large background piece. Place this large background piece over the intersection of the fold lines on the "ring" fabric, matching the finger-pressed center points to the fold lines. Pin the large background piece securely in place on the "ring" fabric.

■ Place the 8 remaining large background pieces at the intersections of the folds and chalk lines on the "ring" fabric.

■ Finger press the center points of the melons and position them between the large background pieces, matching the melon centers to the fold and chalk lines on the "ring" fabric. Also place melons around the outside edges of the large background pieces. Pin the melons in place through all the layers of fabric. Also place

pins around the outer edges of the quilt top.

■ Using a walking or even-feed foot, top stitch the background pieces in place through all the layers of fabric, stitching ¼" in from the raw edges.

Finishing

■ Cut five 3" x 42" binding strips and bind the quilt, referring to "Attaching the Binding" on page 14.

■ Rough up the raw edges of the rings with a small brush with stiff bristles. Clip any long threads or threads that are inhibiting the raveling process. The object is to pull up the seam allowances of the background pieces and create interesting texture. If all of your fabrics are thoroughly preshrunk, you can agitate the quilt in the washer, stopping to clip threads every few minutes, and dry the quilt on the gentle cycle. Touch up the quilt afterwards by steaming it lightly with an iron.

32 Background pieces are stitched along the seam lines and brushed to fray the edges.

■ Add a casing to the top edge of the back side of the quilt, referring to "Adding a Casing" on page 14.

Layered Illusions

Since the Double Wedding Ring pattern is so graphic to begin with, it is fun to add other elements that enhance the illusion of depth and geometric qualities. I chose a background fabric with a lot of flowing lines to contrast with the appliquéd grid lines, which have turned-under edges, although raw edges would work equally well. Using a light-to-dark gradation of colors for the pieced arcs adds another dimensional element that makes this wall quilt one that will get a lot of notice.

Technique: Grid strips over pieced rings

Finished size: 46" square

Note: You can increase the number of grid lines in this quilt; space the strips evenly to look like a garden trellis, and coordinate the look with floral background fabrics.

Fabrics and Supplies*

1 fat quarter (or 19" square) each of eight hand-dyed fabrics in light-to-dark gradations for pieced arcs

1 yard of fabric for background and outer border

1 yard of fabric for grid lines and outer border

1¼ yards of light print fabric for inner border

⅜ yard of fabric for binding

Heavy cardboard

Walking or even-feed foot for machine-guided quilting

*See Resources, pages 94-95

Cut

48 *wedges* each from four colors of hand-dyed fabric (fabrics #3 through #6 from hand-dyed gradations)

48 *end pieces* each, from two colors of hand-dyed fabric (fabrics #2 and #7 from hand-dyed gradations)

24 *corner squares* each from the lightest and darkest two colors of hand-dyed fabric (fabrics #1 and #8 from hand-dyed fabrics)

24 *melons* and 9 *background* large pieces from the background fabric

Seven 2" x 42" strips for the grid lines

Four 3½" x 42" strips for the outer borders

Two 3½" squares for the outer border corner squares from the background fabric

Piecing the Rings

■ Divide the wedge pieces into two stacks. Turn one of the stacks over so you can chain-piece half of the arcs with the lightest value on the left side and the other half with the darkest value on the left side.

■ Sew the end pieces to all the pieced arcs, keeping the color values in order from darkest to lightest.

■ Sew the corner squares onto half of the pieced arcs, keeping the color values in order from darkest to lightest.

■ Sew the pieced arcs to the melons, making sure that one end of both arcs features the dark values and the other end contains the light values.

■ Sew the completed melons to the large background pieces, matching all the values in each intersection.

■ Assemble the 9 rings, referring to "Joining the Rings" on page 12. Lay the elements of each row on a design wall or next to your sewing machine to keep them in order as you sew and take just one background piece and its pieced melons to the sewing machine at a time. Press the joined rings.

■ Turn under and baste ¼" seam allowances on the edges of the joined rings.

Adding the Inner Border

■ Set your sewing machine for a blind-hem stitch with a short stitch length and narrow zigzag width. Lay the rings on the inner border fabric and pin them in place securely.

■ Sew the rings to the border, referring to "Machine Appliquéing the Border" on page 13. Trim away the border fabric underneath the joined rings, leaving a ¼" seam allowance.

■ Trim the outer edges of the border fabric so they are equal in width on all sides of the quilt top. Press the completed quilt top.

Appliquéing the Grid Strips

■ Fold four of the grid strips in half, wrong sides together. Sew a seam ¼" from the raw edges along the length of these strips. Insert a strip of heavy cardboard cut a scant ¾" wide into these fabric tubes, placing the seam allowances at the center on one side. Steam press both sides of the tubes while the cardboard is inside, sliding the cardboard along as you go. Pull out the cardboard after steaming the tubes.

■ Place the quilt top on a design wall. Position the fabric tubes diagonally across the quilt, placing the strips closer together at one corner and farther apart at the other corner. Pin the ends of these strips in place at the edges of the quilt top first, and then pin along the lengths of the strips to keep them straight. Check each grid line with a yardstick to make sure that your grid lines are positioned correctly.

Note: You can also draw chalk guidelines on your completed quilt top and pin the grid strips to the marked lines.

■ Connect the three remaining grid strips end to end with diagonal seams. Then sew them into one long tube and press. Cut this tube in half, creating two grid strips that are long enough to reach across the middle of the quilt top in both directions. Pin these grid strips in place between the previous grid strips, checking to make sure they lie straight.

33 Set your machine to a blind-hem stitch. Appliqué the tubes to the quilt top and press.

Adding the Outer Border
■ Cut four outer border strips to the length of the quilt top. Sew two of these border strips to the top and bottom edges of the quilt.

■ Sew two 3½" squares to each of the remaining two border strips. Sew these borders to the remaining two sides of the quilt top.

Machine Quilting
■ Layer the backing, batting, and quilt top, and baste the layers together with thread or rust-proof safety pins.

■ Using a walking or even-feed foot on your sewing machine, quilt in the seam lines and along the edges of the grid.

Finishing
■ Cut five 2½" x 42" binding strips, and bind the quilt, referring to "Attaching the Binding" on page 14.

■ Add a casing to the top edge of the back side of the quilt. To make a casing for displaying a straight-edged wall quilt, start with a 9" x 42" strip of fabric. Trim the strip to the width of the quilt and hem under 1" at the short ends. Fold the strip in half lengthwise, wrong sides together. Pin and baste the raw edges to the top of the quilt backing, before you stitch the binding to the backing fabric. Hand sew the bottom fold of the casing to the backing; then sew the binding in place, enclosing the top edge of the casing.

Hint of Passion

Hint of Passion was made for a contest that required the use of three colors from a manufacturer's fabric collection. This prescribed coloration occurs in the background of this quilt and in the corner squares. Striped setting fabric and hand-dyed border fabric set off the solid arcs rings, reinforcing the colors of the prints. A wide variety of beads embellish the large background areas, and an irregular pattern of machine-guided quilting fills the border areas. This quilt is from the collection of Sharon Hultgren.

Technique: One-piece arcs

Finished size: 46" square

Double Wedding Ring Quilts: Coming Full Circle – Susan L. Stein

Fabrics and Supplies*

¼ yard each of five hand-dyed fabrics for one-piece arcs

¼ yard each of two fabrics for corner squares in arcs and outer border

One yard of print fabric for background

One yard of striped fabric for inner border and binding

½ yard of fabric for outer border

Assorted decorative beads, such as bugle, teardrop, or stone-like beads

Quilting thread for beading

Walking or even-feed foot for machine-guided quilting

Darning foot for free-motion quilting

*See Resources, pages 94-95

Cut

48 *solid arcs* from the five hand-dyed fabrics. (*Note*: No end pieces are needed for the arcs in this quilt.)

24 *corner squares* each from the two fabrics for corner squares

From one of the two corner square fabrics, cut four 3½" squares for the corner squares in the outer border

9 *background* large pieces and 24 melons from the print fabric

Four 4½" x 42" inner border strips from the striped fabric

Four 3½" x 42" outer border strips from the fabric for the outer border

Piecing the Rings

■ Sew the corner squares to one-half of the one-piece arcs, referring to instructions on "Piecing the Melon Units", page 11.

■ Sew the arcs without corner squares to the melons. Sew the arcs with corner squares to the opposite sides of the melons. Press.

■ Assemble the 9 rings, referring to "Joining the Rings" on page 12. Lay the elements of each row on a design wall or next to your sewing machine to keep them in order as you sew and take just one background piece and its melons to the sewing machine at a time. Press the joined rings. Turn under and baste ¼" on the edges of the rings.

Adding the Inner Border

■ Place the striped inner border strips underneath the edges of the rings; make sure that the strips lie ¼"

under the inner corners of the rings. Line up the stripes exactly the same way on all four sides of the quilt to miter the corners properly. Pin the edges of the joined rings to the inner border strips securely.

■ Set your machine to a blind-hem stitch. Machine appliqué the rings to the border, referring to "Machine Appliquéing the Border" on page 13. Trim away the border fabric underneath the joined rings leaving a ¼" seam allowance.

■ Miter the corner seams of the inner border by folding each border strip over the adjacent border strip at a 45-degree angle, making sure the stripes match exactly. Using blind-hem appliqué, stitch the fold in place at each corner. Trim the mitered seam allowances to ¼" and press.

Adding the Outer Border

■ Cut the four outer border strips to the measurement of the quilt top.

■ Sew two outer border strips to opposite sides of the quilt top, and press.

■ Sew the four corner squares to the remaining two outer border strips and sew them to the remaining two sides of the quilt. Press the completed quilt top.

Machine Quilting

■ Layer the backing, batting, and quilt top, and baste the layers together with thread or rust-proof safety pins.

■ Using a walking or even-feed foot on your sewing machine, quilt in the seam lines of the rings.

■ Quilt a line of large zigzag stitching between the edges of the rings and the outer border, stitching lines by eye, making sure that the corners are stitched neatly.

34 The striped inner border is covered in a bold network of zigzags.

■ Using a walking or even-feed foot on your machine, quilt a cable pattern in the border, turning the corners gracefully by eye.

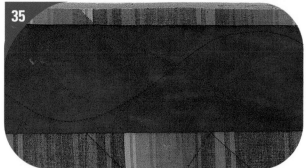

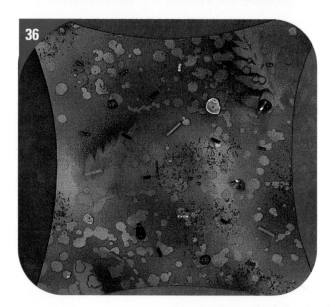

35 The outer border is quilted in a freehand cable pattern using a walking or even-feed foot.

Adding the Beads

■ Using a thin hand-sewing needle, make a knot in the end and slide the needle into a seam allowance, burying the knot. Bring the needle out on top of the quilt and place a bead on the needle and run the needle into the batting.

■ Bring the needle out wherever you want the next bead and stitch it to the quilt in the same manner.

36 Many types of beads add interest and act as the quilting in the background areas.

■ Whenever a strand of thread becomes short, bring the needle through to the back of the quilt, point the needle toward the quilt, and wrap the thread around the needle several times (like a French knot). Stick the needle through the fabric into the batting, and bring the needle out approximately ½" away. Tug on the thread while scraping the knot with your fingernail to pull the knot through the surface and into the batting.

Finishing

■ Cut five 2½" x 42" binding strips and bind the quilt, referring to "Attaching the Binding" on page 14.

■ Add a straight casing to the top edge of the back side of the quilt. To make a casing for displaying a straight-edged wall quilt, start with a 9" x 42" strip of fabric. Trim the strip to the width of the quilt and hem under 1" at the short ends. Fold the strip in half lengthwise, wrong sides together. Pin and baste the raw edges to the top of the quilt backing, before you stitch the binding to the backing fabric. Hand sew the bottom fold of the casing to the backing; then sew the binding in place, enclosing the top edge of the casing.

Poinsettia

Choose a large-scale theme print to set the mood for a festive holiday table topper, or use a Happy Birthday theme fabric for making a table runner for a loved one's special day. The wedges in the pieced arcs can be coordinating prints, or solid fabrics, as I used in my Christmas quilt. These long, narrow quilts make great table runners and door banners, as well as perfect gifts for almost any special occasion.

Technique: Highlighting theme fabrics   Finished size: Approximately 18" x 60"

Double Wedding Ring Quilts: Coming Full Circle – Susan L. Stein   49

Fabrics and Supplies*

¼ yard each of eight fabrics for wedges, end pieces, and corner squares

⅔ to 1 yard of large-scale theme print fabric for background (Increase this amount, if necessary, to fussy cut printed motifs.)

1 yard of fabric for border

⅓ yard of fabric for binding

Walking or even-feed foot for machine-guided quilting

*See Resources, pages 94-95

Cut

32 *wedge* pieces each from four colors of fabric

32 *end pieces* each from two colors of fabric

16 *corner squares* each from two colors of fabric

16 *melons* and 5 *background* large pieces from the theme print fabric, highlighting printed motifs as desired

Cut the border fabric in half across the 42" width and sew the short ends of the two pieces together to make an 18"x 80" long piece. Press the seam open.

Piecing the Rings

■ Sew the sixteen melon units, referring to the photo on page 12 and "Piecing the Melon Units" on page 11, and press. If you are using light to dark values of red and green as I did in the quilt shown on page 49, decide whether you want to place the light values at the ends of the arcs or in the center of the arcs.

■ Assemble the five rings, referring to "Joining the Rings" on page 12. Lay the elements of each row on a design wall or next to your sewing machine to keep them in order as you sew and take just one background piece and its pieced melons to the sewing machine at a time. Press the joined rings.

■ Turn under and baste ¼" on the edges of the rings, rounding out the corner squares on the corners of the quilt top.

Adding the Border

■ Place the border fabric right side up on a table. Position the joined rings on the border fabric so the seam of the border fabric matches the center point of the middle ring, and pin the rings in place securely on the border fabric. Trim away the excess border fabric.

■ Set your machine to a blind-hem stitch. Machine appliqué the rings to the border fabric, referring to "Machine Appliquéing the Border" on page 14. Trim away the border fabric underneath the joined rings, leaving a ¼" seam allowance. Press the completed quilt top.

Machine Quilting

■ Layer the backing, batting, and quilt top, and baste the layers together with thread or rust-proof safety pins.

■ Using a walking or even-feed foot on your sewing machine, quilt in the seam lines of the rings.

Finishing

■ Trim the backing fabric and batting to ¼" from the edges of the quilt top.

■ Cut four 2" x 42" binding strips from the theme print fabric and bind the quilt, referring to "Attaching the Binding" on page 14.

■ Add a casing to the top edge of the back side of the quilt, referring to "Adding a Casing" on page 14, so the quilt can be used either as a door banner or a table runner.

Japanese Chrysanthemums

The starting point for this elegant wallhanging was three wonderful overdyed silk kimono panels. The dark red panel became the background pieces for the three rings and an embroidered portion of the same fabric was used for the side and bottom sections on the left. Another kimono panel was used for the border at the right side, and a partial third panel was cut for the melons and the small section at the top of the quilt. The elements in this piece are placed in a formal and asymmetrical arrangement, and, in keeping with the banner format, I did not use batting or binding.

Technique: Silk kimono panels and beading   Finished size: 25" x 52"

Double Wedding Ring Quilts: Coming Full Circle – Susan L. Stein   51

Note: Exact yardages are not listed for this project because the fabrics you have available will determine the configuration of the borders and the length of your wallhanging.

Fabrics and Supplies*

Two main silk kimono panels for background
Silk kimono panel for melons and small area above rings
1/8 yard each of two fabrics for corner squares
1/3 yard each of two solid fabrics for one-piece rings
Woven cotton or nylon tricot fusible interfacing
Bugle beads
Thin beading needle
Walking or even-feed foot for machine-guided quilting
Darning foot for free-motion quilting
*See Resources, pages 94-95

Cut

20 *solid arcs* from the hand-dyed cotton fabrics
10 *melon* pieces from silk kimono fabric
3 *background* large pieces from silk kimono fabric
8 *corner squares* from one corner square fabric
12 *corner squares* from the other corner square fabric

Piecing the Rings

■ Piece the 10 melon units, referring to the photos and instructions on pages 11-13 for "Piecing the Melon Units." Press the melon units.

■ Assemble the 3 rings, referring to "Joining the Rings" on page 12. Lay the elements of each row on a design wall or next to your sewing machine to keep them in order as you sew and take just one background piece and its pieced melons to the sewing machine at a time. I used one corner square fabric at both ends of the vertical melons and the other corner fabric for the horizontal melons to create a more formal look.

■ If the interfaced silk is thick, press the seam allowances away from the background fabric instead of toward it. Press the joined rings.

■ Turn under and baste 1/4" on the edges of the rings, rounding out the corner squares on the corners of the quilt top.

Adding the Rings to the Kimono Panels

■ Lay the remaining portion of one silk kimono panel and the silk kimono panel for the right side of the quilt on a table to create an interesting framework for the rings. Add extra sections of silk fabric, if you wish. Sew the panels together where they meet, placing right sides together and using a 1/4" seam allowance. It is not necessary to have a complete panel underneath the area where the rings will lie. Pin the basted rings in the desired position.

■ Set your sewing machine to a blind-hem stitch. Machine appliqué the rings to the border, referring to "Machine Appliquéing the Border" on page 13. Trim away the border fabric underneath the joined rings leaving a 1/4" seam allowance.

■ Press the completed quilt top.

Machine Quilting

■ Measure the quilt top and cut a piece of backing fabric that is slightly wider and 1" longer. Cut the backing in half. Using a 1/4" seam allowance, sew the two backing pieces together, leaving an 8" opening in the middle for turning the quilt right side out later.

■ Place the pieced backing right sides together with the pieced quilt top and pin them together around the edges. Using a walking or even-feed foot on your sewing machine and a 1/4" seam allowance, sew all the way around the edges. Trim the excess backing fabric and corners. Turn the quilt right side out through the opening in the center backing seam. Hand sew the opening closed, and press.

■ Quilt in the ditch of the seam lines.

■ Change to a darning foot and lower or cover the feed dogs on your sewing machine. Free-motion quilt the background areas in a pattern of freeform "chrysanthemums."

37 Free-motion quilting in the large background areas complements the designs in the silk kimono fabric.

Adding the Beads

■ Thread a very thin hand-sewing needle with thread for beading and make a knot in the end. Add bugle beads through both layers of the quilt or simply tack the layers of fabric together with thread from the back side of the quilt.

■ Since there is no batting to support the weight of the fabrics in this quilt, take care to add enough beads to anchor the layers together evenly throughout the border areas.

38 Bugle beads hold the layers together outside the rings without distracting from the printed designs on the silk fabric.

Finishing

■ For a wall quilt with no binding, cut a 9" x 42" strip of fabric and trim it to fit the back of the quilt. Hem the short ends and sew the raw edges together, with the right sides of the fabric together. Then turn the tube right side out and press it, positioning the seam along the center on one side. Hand sew the pressed casing to the top edge of the quilt backing, stitching both of the long edges.

River of Gold

This quilt incorporates a 36" square pictorial panel fabric into a rainbow of light, medium, and dark Double Wedding Rings. I used a larger printed landscape panel and cut away the bottom of the scene so it would work with nine rings.

Technique: Landscape background with rainbow rings

Finished size: 42" square

Double Wedding Ring Quilts: Coming Full Circle – Susan L. Stein

Fabrics and Supplies*

24 fat quarters of gray, blue, green, yellow, orange, red,
  purple, and blue-green print fabric, choosing 1 light,
  1 medium, and 1 dark value of each color

36" square printed landscape panel for background

1¼ yards of fabric for border

½ yard of fabric for binding

Walking or even-feed foot for machine-guided quilting

Darning foot for free-motion quilting

*See Resources, pages 94-95

Cut

From the eight light-value fat quarters:

17 *wedge* pieces each from the light green, yellow,
orange, and red fabrics

17 *end pieces* each from the light-value blue and purple fabrics

9 *corner squares* each from the light-value gray and
blue-green fabrics

From the eight medium-value fat quarters:

14 *wedge* pieces each from the medium-value green,
yellow, orange, and red fabrics

14 *end pieces* each from the medium-value blue and
purple fabrics

6 *corner squares* each from the medium-value gray and
blue-green fabrics

From the eight dark-value fat quarters:

17 *wedge* pieces each from the dark-value green, yellow,
orange, and red fabrics

17 *end pieces* each from the dark-value blue and purple fabrics

9 *corner squares* each from the dark-value gray and
blue-green fabrics

24 *melons* and 9 *background* large pieces from the 36"
printed landscape panel. Place the cut pieces on a
design wall to keep the landscape sections in order.

Piecing the Rings

■ Sew 17 arcs from the light-value wedges and end
pieces, referring to the photo on page 55 and "Piecing
the Melon Units" on page 11, and press. Add light-
value gray and blue-green corner squares to the ends of
9 of these light-colored arcs.

■ Sew 14 arcs from the medium-value wedges and end
pieces in the same manner. Add medium-value corner
squares to 6 of these medium-colored arcs.

■ Sew 17 arcs from the dark-value wedges and end
pieces in the same manner. Add dark value corner
squares to 9 of these dark-colored arcs.

■ Place the large background pieces and melons on
a design wall.

Note: Keep in mind that the top row of rings contains light values, the middle row consists of medium values, and the bottom row is dark in value.

■ Assemble the 9 rings. To sew the melon units to
the large background pieces, begin by finger creasing
the center points on the four curved edges on a large
background piece. Match and pin the center seam of
a pieced arc in a melon unit to a center point on the
large background piece. Place another pin ¼" in
from the point of the large background piece; then
insert the pin into the seam between the end piece
and corner square of the pieced arc underneath.
Pinch the fabrics together on the pin and then
anchor the pin securely in the fabrics, as shown.
Repeat this process at the other point of the large
background piece.

■ Continue to add complete melons to the sides of the
large background pieces as needed for your project,
making sure there are no two corner squares touching
that are the same fabric. Press the seam allowances
toward the background pieces. Press as you go.

Note: The corner squares will be left hanging free. Sew
this seam with the large background piece on top,
backstitching at both ends.

■ Remove one section at a time from the design wall as
you sew and take just one background piece and its
pieced melons to the sewing machine at a time. Press
the joined rings.

■ Turn under and baste ¼" on the edges of the rings.

Adding the Border

■ Set your sewing machine for a blind-hem stitch with a
short stitch length and narrow zigzag width. Lay the
rings on the border fabric and pin them in place securely.

■ Sew the rings to the border, and trim away the border fabric underneath the joined rings leaving a ¼" seam allowance.

■ Trim the outer edges of the border fabric so they are equal in width on all sides of the quilt top. Press.

Machine Quilting

■ Layer the backing, batting, and quilt top, and baste the layers together with thread or rust-proof safety pins.

■ Using a walking or even-feed foot on your sewing machine, quilt in the seam lines of the rings.

39 Background quilting follows the lines in the landscape print.

■ Change to a darning foot and lower or cover the feed dogs on your sewing machine. Quilt around the landscape motifs. Stipple quilt the border.

40 The border fabric carries out the landscape theme and is simply stipple-quilted.

Finishing

■ Trim the backing fabric and batting to ¼" from the edges of the quilt top.

■ Cut five 2½" x 42" binding strips and bind the quilt, referring to "Attaching the Binding" on page 14.

■ Add a casing to the top edge of the back side of the quilt. To make a casing for displaying a straight-edged wall quilt, start with a 9" x 42" strip of fabric. Trim the strip to the width of the quilt and hem under 1" at the short ends. Fold the strip in half lengthwise, wrong sides together. Pin and baste the raw edges to the top of the quilt backing, before you stitch the binding to the backing fabric. Hand sew the bottom fold of the casing to the backing; then sew the binding in place, enclosing the top edge of the casing.

If you love satin-stitch or fused appliqué, you could also create your own original landscape panel.

Nasturtiums

Piecing two groups of arcs, one with the dark values on the left end and the other with the dark values on the right end, allows you to create a dramatic wallhanging that pulses with light. Look for a background print fabric to complement the solid colors of the rings and a bright accent color for the setting fabric behind them.

Technique: Light-to-dark pieced arcs

Finished size: 46" x 57"

Fabrics and Supplies*

1 fat quarter (or 19" square) each of eight hand-dyed fabrics in light-to-dark gradation for pieced arcs

1 yard of floral print fabric for the background

1½ yards of bright fabric for setting fabric behind rings

⅝ yard of dark fabric for inner border and binding

¾ yard of medium fabric for pieced outer border or a

1¾ yard-length for an outer border with no seams

Walking or even-feed foot for machine-guided quilting

Darning foot for free-motion quilting

*See Resources, pages 94-95

Cut

62 *wedges* each from four colors of the hand-dyed fabric (values #3 through #6 in a hand-dyed bundle)

62 *end pieces* each from two colors of the hand-dyed fabric (values #2 and #7 in a hand-dyed bundle)

31 *corner squares* each from two colors of the hand-dyed fabric (values #1 and #8 or the lightest and darkest colors in a hand-dyed bundle)

12 *background* large pieces and 31 melons from the print fabric for the background

Piecing the Rings

■ Divide the wedge pieces into two piles. Turn one of the piles over and chain-piece one half of the arcs with the darkest value on the left side and one half with the darkest value on the right side.

■ Sew the end pieces to all of the arcs, keeping the color values in order.

■ Add the corner squares onto half of the pieced arcs, keeping the color values in order.

■ Arrange the print background pieces and melons on a design wall so the motifs are distributed evenly and right side up inside each ring.

■ Place the arcs next to the large background pieces and melons on the design wall so one intersection is all light corner squares, and the next intersection is all dark corner squares, referring to the photo on page 57.

■ Sew the melon units, referring to the photos and instructions on pages 11-13 for "Piecing the Melon Units," and press.

■ Assemble the 12 rings, referring to "Joining the Rings" on page 12. Lay the elements of each row next to your sewing machine to keep them in order and take just one background piece and its pieced melons to the sewing machine at a time. Press the joined rings. Turn under and baste ¼" on the edges of the rings.

Adding the Setting Fabric

■ Set your machine to a blind-hem stitch. Lay the rings on the setting fabric and pin them in place securely. Trim the setting fabric to ½" away from the outside the rings, making sure that the quilt top is square. There will be only ¼" of setting fabric showing at the fullest part the rings after the outer border is added.

■ Machine appliqué the rings to the setting fabric, referring to "Machine Appliquéing the Border" on page 13. Trim away the setting fabric underneath the joined rings leaving a ¼" seam allowance, and press.

Adding the Inner Border

■ Cut five 1" x 42" strips of fabric for the inner border. Measure your quilt top horizontally through the center, and cut two strips to this measurement. Sew these strips to the top and bottom edges of the setting fabric, and press.

■ Measure your quilt top vertically through the center to determine the length for the side borders for your quilt. Sew three strips of inner border fabric together end-to-end, and cut the two side borders from this pieced strip. Sew these strips to the sides of the setting fabric, and press.

Adding the Outer Border

■ Cut five 4½" x 42" strips of outer border fabric. Measure your quilt top horizontally through the center, and cut two of these strips to this measurement. Sew these strips to the top and bottom edges of the inner border, and press.

■ Measure your quilt top vertically through the center to determine the length for the side outer borders for your quilt. Sew three strips of outer border fabric end-to-end, and cut the two side outer borders from this pieced strip. Sew these strips to side edges of the inner border, and press.

Machine Quilting

■ Layer the backing, batting, and quilt top, and baste the layers together with thread or rust-proof safety pins.

■ Using a walking or even-feed foot on your sewing machine, machine quilt in the seam lines of the arcs, continuing across the background.

41 Quilt vertical wavy lines in the borders, through the short seam lines in the middle of the arcs, and across the large background pieces.

Finishing

■ Trim the backing fabric and batting to ½" from the edges of the quilt top.

■ Cut six 2½" x 42" binding strips and bind the quilt, referring to "Attaching the Binding" on page 14.

■ Add a casing to the top edge of the back side of the quilt. To make a casing for displaying a straight-edged wall quilt, start with a 9" x 42" strip of fabric. Trim the strip to the width of the quilt and hem under 1" at the short ends. Fold the strip in half lengthwise, wrong sides together. Pin and baste the raw edges to the top of the quilt backing, before you stitch the binding to the backing fabric. Hand sew the bottom fold of the casing to the backing; then sew the binding in place, enclosing the top edge of the casing.

Double Wedding Ring Quilts: Coming Full Circle – Susan L. Stein

Marble Floor

Start with a multicolored print and choose coordinating fabrics for the rings, melons, and Nine-Patch in this quilt. Make sure there is good contrast between the individual wedges as well as between the two Nine-Patch fabrics, and between the pieced arcs and the Nine-Patches.

Technique: Nine-patch background

Finished size: 40" square

Double Wedding Ring Quilts: Coming Full Circle – Susan L. Stein

Fabrics and Supplies

$\frac{1}{3}$ yard each of 6 fabrics for wedges and end pieces

$\frac{1}{4}$ yard each of two fabrics for corner squares

$\frac{5}{8}$ yard each of one light and one dark fabric for Nine-Patch centers

$\frac{1}{2}$ yard of fabric for melons

$\frac{5}{8}$ yard of striped fabric for border

$\frac{3}{8}$ yard of fabric for binding

Walking or even-feed foot for machine-guided quilting

Cut

48 *wedges* each from the four wedge fabrics

48 *end pieces* each from the two end piece fabrics

24 *corner squares* each from the two corner square fabrics

24 *melons.*

45 *squares*, $3\frac{1}{2}$" each, from the dark Nine-Patch fabric

36 *squares*, $3\frac{1}{2}$" each, from the light Nine-Patch fabric

Four $4\frac{1}{2}$" x 42" strips from the border fabric

Note: In this quilt, the melons are cut from a different fabric than the large background pieces. Cut a few pieces of each shape and place them on the wall so you can see the effect of the color choices from a distance. It is better to audition the fabrics before you spend any time sewing or before you waste a fabric that doesn't work.

Piecing the Rings

■ Piece 9 Nine-Patch blocks from the 36 light and 45 dark squares, placing the dark squares in the corners and center of the blocks. Press well. Carefully cut 9 large background pieces from the Nine-Patch blocks.

■ Sew the 24 melon units. Lay the pieced melon units and the large background pieces on a design wall in the arrangement specified in the project instructions. Then follow these steps to join the rings together.

■ To sew the melon units to the large background pieces, begin by finger creasing the center points on the four curved edges on a large background piece. Match and pin the center seam of a pieced arc in a melon unit to a center point on the large background piece. Place another pin $\frac{1}{4}$" in from the point of the large background piece; then insert the pin into the seam between the end piece and corner square of the pieced arc underneath. Pinch the fabrics together on the pin and then anchor the pin securely in the fabrics, as shown. Repeat this process at the other point of the large background piece. *Note:* The corner squares will be left hanging free. Sew this seam with the large background piece on top, backstitching at both ends.

■ Continue to add complete melons to the sides of the large background pieces as needed for your project, making sure there are no two corner squares that are the same fabric touching. Press the seam allowances toward the background pieces. Press as you go.

■ Sew the corner squares together to complete the rings, beginning at the raw edges and backstitching at the end of the seam, and press.

■ Assemble the 9 rings, referring to "Joining the Rings" on page 12. Lay the elements of each row on a design wall or next to your sewing machine to keep them in order as you sew, and take just one background piece and its pieced melons to the sewing machine at a time. Press the joined rings.

■ To join the rows of pieced rings together, start by sewing the middle ring in each row together, and work outward in both directions from there. When you have joined the rows of rings, go back and sew all of the pairs of corner squares together. When sewing the corner squares together on the outside edges, backstitch at the raw edges so the seam allowances remain free for sewing the rings to the border. Press the seam allowances toward the background.

■ Turn under and baste $\frac{1}{4}$" on the edges of the rings.

Adding the Border

■ Place the four 4½" x 42" border strips under the edges of the joined rings, making sure that there is a ¼" seam allowance underneath the inner corners. If you are using a striped fabric, line up the stripes carefully on all four sides to properly miter the corners. Pin the rings to the border strips.

■ Set your machine to a blind-hem stitch. Lay the rings on the border fabric and pin them in place. Trim the border fabric evenly around the outside of the rings.

■ Sew the rings to the border, referring to "Machine Appliquéing the Border," page 13. Trim away border fabric underneath the rings leaving a ¼" seam allowance.

■ Miter the border corner seams by folding one border strip over the adjacent border strip at a 45-degree angle, making sure that the stripes match. Using the blind-hem stitch, appliqué the fold in place. Trim the mitered seam allowances to ¼" and press quilt top.

Machine Quilting

■ Layer the backing, batting, and quilt top, and baste the layers together with thread or rust-proof pins.

■ Using a walking or even-feed foot on your sewing machine, quilt in the seam lines of the rings. Also quilt in the seam lines of the Nine-Patches, extending the lines through the arcs, melons, and borders.

42 Quilting lines follow seam lines across the Nine-Patches and arcs.

Finishing

■ Trim the backing fabric and batting even with the edges of the quilt top.

■ Cut five 2½" x 42" binding strips and bind the quilt, referring to "Attaching the Binding" on page 14.

■ Add a casing to the top edge of the back side of the quilt, referring to "Adding a Casing" on page 14.

Climbing Roses

This project is for the romantic in you. Hand-dyed fabrics create a soft look that puts the visual emphasis on the appliqué and quilting. The flower petals are lined, so they stand out from the surface of the quilt, and the bias tube is easy to construct – no turning involved! For ideas in designing flower shapes, look at books on Baltimore Album quilts and Japanese folded flowers. (I once put poppies on a vine and of course I received comments from flower experts!)

Technique: Three-dimensional appliqués

Finished size: 41" square

Fabrics and Supplies*

⅓ yard each of eight fabrics for wedges, end pieces, corner squares, petals, buds, calyxes, and leaves, or 1 fat-quarter bundle of hand-dyed fabric in eight shades

Note: If you choose to make a pieced binding as shown in the quilt on page 63, purchase two fat-quarter bundles or one half-yard bundle of hand-dyed fabric.

1 yard of fabric for background and petal linings

1 yard of fabric for border

1 yard of fabric for bias vine

½ yard of fabric for binding (if not piecing the binding)

¼"-wide metal or plastic bias press bar for bias tubes (or make one from heavy cardboard)

60" metal ruler (optional)

24" acrylic ruler

Template plastic or cardboard

Chalk pencil

Yellow embroidery floss

Embroidery and hand-appliqué needles

Walking or even-feed foot for machine-guided quilting

Darning foot for free-motion quilting

*See Resources, pages 94-95

Cut

48 *wedges* each from four colors of the hand-dyed fabric (values #3 through #6 in a hand-dyed bundle)

48 *end pieces* each from two colors of the hand-dyed fabric (values #2 and #7 in a hand-dyed bundle)

24 *corner squares* each from two colors of the hand-dyed fabric (values #1 and #8 in a hand-dyed bundle).

24 *melons* and nine large background pieces from the background fabric

Four 5" x 42" strips of border fabric

Four 5" squares of background fabric for the border corners

Piecing the Rings

■ Sew the 24 melon units, referring to the photos and instructions on pages 11-13 for "Piecing the Melon Units," and press.

■ Assemble the 9 rings, referring to "Joining the Rings" on page 12. Lay the elements of each row on a design wall or next to your sewing machine to keep them in order as you sew, and take just one background piece and its pieced melons to the sewing machine at a time. Press the joined rings.

■ Turn under and baste ¼" on the edges of the rings, rounding out the four outer pairs of corner squares.

Adding the Border

■ Measure the basted rings from corner square seam to corner square seam. Cut the four border strips to that length, adding ½" for seam allowances.

■ Sew the corner squares to the ends of two border strips. Sew the border strips with corner squares to the outer border strips without squares, creating a frame-like square border.

■ Lay the border on a table and position the rings on top, matching the seams between the corner squares of the joined rings to the inner corners of the border squares, and making sure that the edges of the border strips extend ¼" underneath the rings. Pin the rings to the border securely.

■ Set your machine to a blind-hem stitch. Machine appliqué the rings to the border, referring to "Machine Appliquéing the Border" on page 13. Trim away the border fabric underneath the joined rings, leaving a ¼" seam allowance.

■ Press the completed quilt top.

Adding the Vine

■ Press the vine fabric and lay it flat on a table. Using the 60" metal ruler and a rotary cutter, cut the fabric diagonally from corner to corner, creating a true bias edge.

■ Lay the 24" acrylic ruler over the vine fabric to align the 1" line with the cut bias edge. Place the long metal ruler flush to the edge of the acrylic ruler and remove the shorter ruler to cut a 1"-wide bias strip. Continue to cut bias strips until you have 5 yards total length.

■ Sew the bias strips end-to-end and press the seam allowances open. Fold the bias strip lengthwise with wrong sides together, and sew a ³⁄₁₆" seam, being careful not to stretch the bias strip as it goes under the presser foot. Trim the seam allowance in half.

■ Insert a bias press bar into the bias tube so the trimmed seam allowance lies on one side. Press the bias tube, sliding the press bar through the tube as you go.

■ Hang the quilt top on a design wall. Beginning at the bottom edge of the quilt top, draw a chalk line where you want the vine to be.

■ Hand appliqué the vine over the chalk; skip from one side to the other, so you can stitch the inside curves first and make sure that the bias tube lies flat. (See Resources, page 92, Books, for book resources on hand appliqué, and those on Baltimore Albums and Japanese folded flowers.)

Adding the Flowers and Leaves

■ The three-dimensional roses in this quilt are made up of a darker bottom layer, a medium-value inner layer, and a lighter top layer of petals, all of which are faced with a lining of the darkest fabric used in the rose. Trace the flower, bud, calyx, and leaf patterns from page 68 onto template plastic or cardboard.

■ Divide the leftover pieces of the fat quarters, vine fabric, and background fabric into leaf and flower colors. Choose the fabrics you want to use for the lining and tops of the large, medium, and small petal shapes, the calyxes, buds, and the leaves.

■ Place the lining fabric right sides together with the top fabric for the large petal shape. (I used the darkest color for the lining and also for the top fabric.) Place the large petal shape template on the fabric and mark around it. Using scissors, cut out the largest petal shape through both layers of fabric, adding the seam allowance by eye as you cut. Make a total of 5 of these large petal shapes.

■ Place the lining fabric right sides together with the top fabric for the medium-size petal shape and cut out five medium petal shapes and linings in the same manner as for the large petal shapes.

■ Place the lining fabric right sides together with the top fabric for the smallest petal shape and cut out five small petal shapes and linings in the same manner as for the large and medium petal shapes.

■ With the top and lining pieces for each petal shape right sides together, sew on the marked lines, using a short stitch length on your sewing machine. Trim the seam allowances on each petal shape to $\frac{1}{8}$", and clip the inner corners and curves. Cut a 1" slit at the middle of the lining pieces; turn the petal shapes right side out through these slits, using a stick or point turner to push out the petals and create smooth curves. Press the completed petal shapes lightly.

■ To make a three-dimensional rose, stack 1 large, 1 medium, and 1 small petal shape on top of each other, staggering the petals to make the flower look full. Repeat this process for all 5 roses. Arrange the roses on the quilt top, but do not attach them permanently at this time.

43 The roses are made of three lined petal shapes that are sewn onto the quilt with French knots.

■ Cut three 3" circles of a flower color for the buds. Cut 3 calyx pieces from a leaf color, adding seam allowances by eye as you cut.

■ Fold the circles in half with the wrong sides together. Fold the half-circles into thirds, creating a bud with a pointed top and curved bottom edge. Using a hand-sewing needle and a double strand of cotton thread, do a line of running stitches along the curved bottom edges of the buds through all the layers of fabric. Pull

up the stitches to gather the bottom edges of the buds and knot and cut the thread.

■ Pin the three buds to the quilt top, referring to the photo on page 63, and cover the gathered edges with the calyx pieces. Hand appliqué the calyxes in place over the buds, enclosing the gathered edges of the buds.

44 The buds are folded circles gathered into the appliquéd calyxes.

■ Mark and cut out a selection of leaves in both sizes. Pin the leaves onto the quilt top, referring to the photo on page 63 for placement guidance. Remove the roses temporarily, and hand appliqué the leaves onto the quilt top. *Note*: You can also trim some of the leaves for this quilt to customize the shapes.

■ Press the completed quilt top.

Machine Quilting

■ Layer the backing, batting, and quilt top, and baste the layers together with thread or rust-proof safety pins.

■ Using a walking or even-feed foot on your sewing machine, quilt in the seam lines of the pieced rings.

■ Using a darning foot on your sewing machine, free-motion quilt veins into the leaves. Stipple quilt the background to highlight the leaves and buds.

■ Free-motion quilt a leafy vine around the border, filling the areas around the rings evenly with clusters of 6 to 10 leaves; begin some with a few berries and end with a tendril. This prevents straining the wrists and allows you to breathe and reposition your hands.

45 The border is quilted with free-motion leaves and vines that are custom-fit to the contours of the rings.

■ Free-motion quilt the border corner squares in a pattern of leaves and vines that coordinates well with the border quilting.

46 The corner squares are quilted with matching thread in a leaf and vine design to match the borders.

Finishing

■ Using an embroidery needle threaded with three strands of the embroidery floss, sew the roses onto the quilt with a circle of French knots covering the entire center area. This will pull up the petals, making them look even more three-dimensional.

■ To make the pieced binding strips for this quilt, measure your quilt through the center in both directions. Take the shorter of these two measurements, and divide it by 16. Add ½" to this number and cut two strips this width from each of the 8 arc colors. Sew eight of these strips together, side by side, maintaining the order of colors, using a ¼" seam allowance. Repeat for the second set of eight strips. Press these seam allowances open.

■ Cut nine 2½"-wide crosswise slices from the strip sets. Sew two slices end-to-end, creating one pieced binding strip for each side of the quilt. Remove the end rectangles from the ninth strip and cut them in half. Sew these pieces to the ends of two of the four binding strips, matching colors, so the binding strips will be long enough to turn under at the corners of the quilt.

■ Press the pieced binding strips in half with wrong sides together. Bind the top and bottom edges of the quilt first using the two shorter binding strips; then bind the sides of the quilt using the two longer binding strips.

■ Add a casing to the top edge of the back side of the quilt, referring to "Adding a Casing" on page 14.

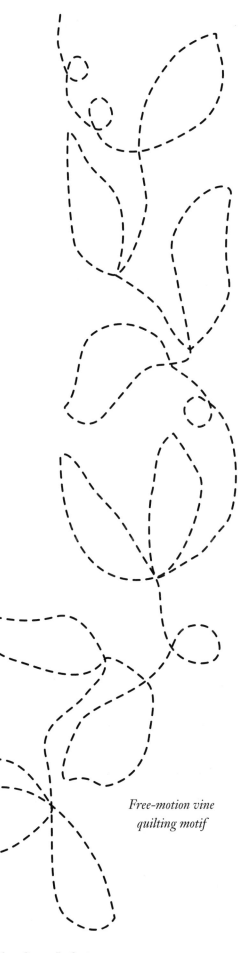

Free-motion vine quilting motif

Three-dimensional rose templates

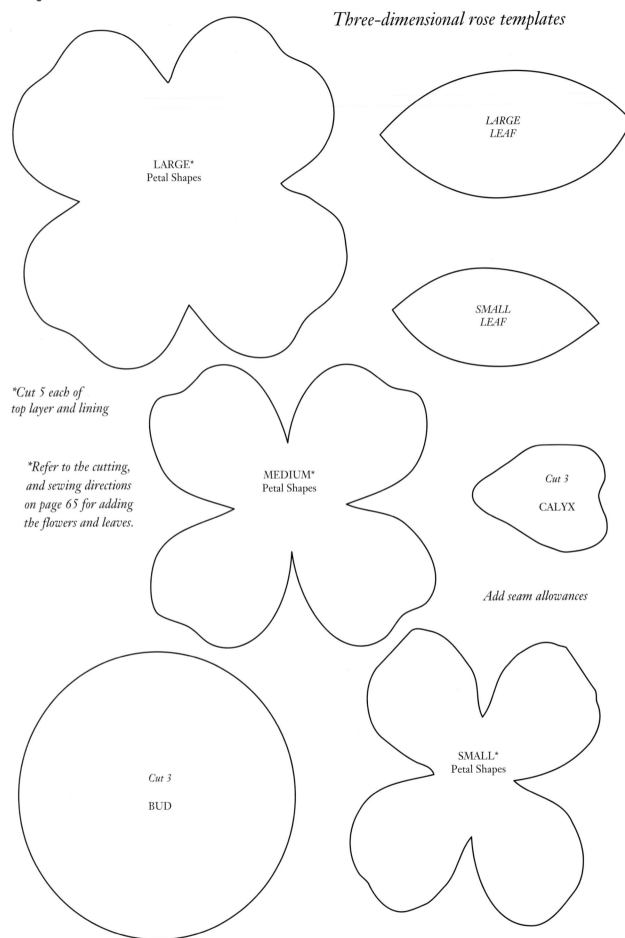

LARGE*
Petal Shapes

LARGE
LEAF

SMALL
LEAF

*Cut 5 each of
top layer and lining

*Refer to the cutting,
and sewing directions
on page 65 for adding
the flowers and leaves.

MEDIUM*
Petal Shapes

Cut 3

CALYX

Add seam allowances

Cut 3

BUD

SMALL*
Petal Shapes

Country Plaids and Stripes

For a relaxed country look, make a Double Wedding Ring in woven plaids and stripes. If you use a template system to cut your wedges, the lines of the plaids and stripes will be randomly placed, giving your quilt a more primitive look. This wallhanging is machine quilted with the traditional spiderweb motif in the large background areas, and free-motion quilted vines in the border. For an "instant antique" look, wash your finished quilt in warm water and dry it on the hot setting in your clothes dryer. Even if all the fabrics are preshrunk, they will still shrink more, taking on an old, puckered appearance.

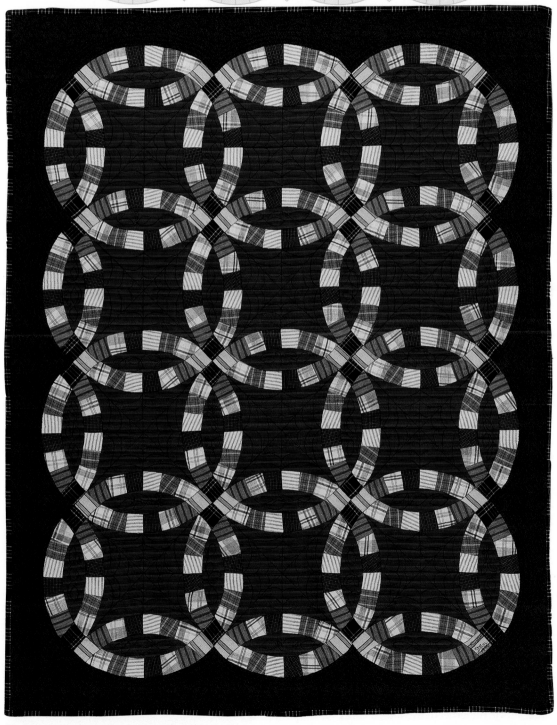

Technique: Using plaid and striped fabrics

Finished size: 42" x 52"

Double Wedding Ring Quilts: Coming Full Circle – Susan L. Stein

Fabrics and Supplies*

⅓ yard each of six plaid and striped fabrics in contrasing colors for wedges and end pieces

¼ yard each of two plaid or striped fabrics for corner squares

1 yard of striped fabric for background

1⅔ yards of fabric for border

½ yard of fabric for binding

Tracing paper

Walking or even-feed foot for machine-guided quilting

Darning foot for free-motion quilting

*See Resources, pages 94-95

Cut

62 *wedges* each from the four fabrics for wedges

62 *end pieces* each from two fabrics for end pieces

31 *corner squares* each from two fabrics for corner squares

12 *large background* pieces and 31 *melons* from the background fabric

Piecing the Rings

■ Sew the 31 melon units, referring to the photos and instructions on pages 11-13 for "Piecing the Melon Units."

■ Assemble the 12 rings, see "Joining the Rings" on page 12, keeping the background stripe aligned the same way in each piece. Press. Lay the elements of each row on a design wall or next to your sewing machine to keep them in order as you sew and take just one background piece and its pieced melons to the sewing machine at a time. Press the joined rings.

■ Turn under and baste ¼" on the edges of the rings, rounding out the four outer pairs of corner squares.

Adding the Border

■ Set your machine to a blind-hem stitch. Lay the rings on the border fabric and pin them in place securely. Trim the border fabric evenly all the way around the outside of the rings.

■ Machine appliqué the rings to the border, referring to "Machine Appliquéing the Border" on page 13. Trim away the border fabric underneath the joined rings, leaving a ¼" seam allowance. Press the completed quilt top.

Machine Quilting

■ Layer the backing, batting, and quilt top, and baste the layers together with thread or rust-proof safety pins.

■ To create the spider web quilting pattern, use a chalk pencil to draw diagonal lines from point to point on the large background pieces. Then draw horizontal and vertical lines through the centers of the background pieces. Using a walking or even-feed foot on your sewing machine, quilt on the drawn lines, starting and ending with tiny stitches to fasten the thread. Clip the threads close to the surface of the quilt.

■ Change to a darning foot and lower or cover the feed dogs on your sewing machine. Connect the straight lines in the large background pieces with free-motion, curved quilting lines that look like a spider web, going around the web three times. If you prefer to make the web look uniform, you can draw the design on a sheet of white paper, using the pattern on page 71. When you have created a spider web design you like, trace it onto as many pieces of tracing paper as there are large background pieces in your quilt. Pin the tracing paper designs over the background areas and stitch through the paper. Remove the paper after you finish quilting.

47 Spider webs are a traditional quilting design for the Double Wedding Ring pattern.

Note: Don't worry about making the spider webs in your quilt look symmetrical – a real spider doesn't!

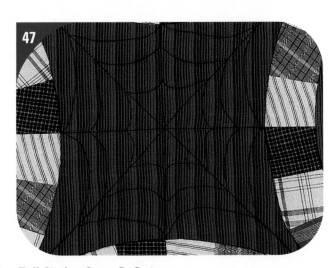

48 The melons are filled with free-motion leaves and vines motifs.

■ In the borders, free-motion quilt three lines, echoing the edge of the rings. Then add continuous-line quilting in a vine and leaf pattern, filling in the inside corners on the rings and the outside corners. I like to end the vine with a tendril or bunch of berries every few inches to allow myself a chance to breathe and reposition my hands.

49 The echo quilting lines in the border follow the contours of the rings.

Note: I recommend using quilting gloves to help in maneuvering the quilt without straining the wrists.

Finishing
■ Trim the backing fabric and batting to ¼" from the edges of the quilt top.

■ Cut five 2½" x 42" binding strips and bind the quilt, referring to "Attaching the Binding" on page 14.

■ Add a casing to the top edge of the back side of the quilt, referring to "Adding a Casing" on page 14.

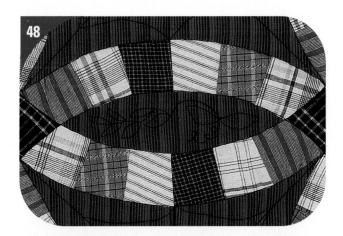

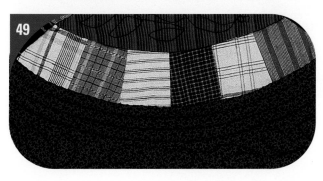

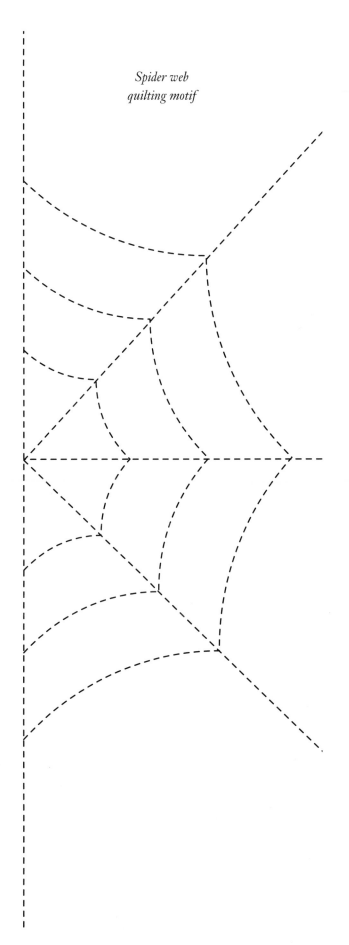

Spider web quilting motif

Prickly Purple

Collect all your scraps or select an assortment of colorful fat quarters for this simple quilt with "prickly" Prairie Points and "thorn" quilting in the large background areas. Notice how different this scrappy approach is from other quilts in this book that feature hand-dyed fabrics. Make sure that the fabrics you choose for the Prairie Points contrast with the ring and border fabrics.

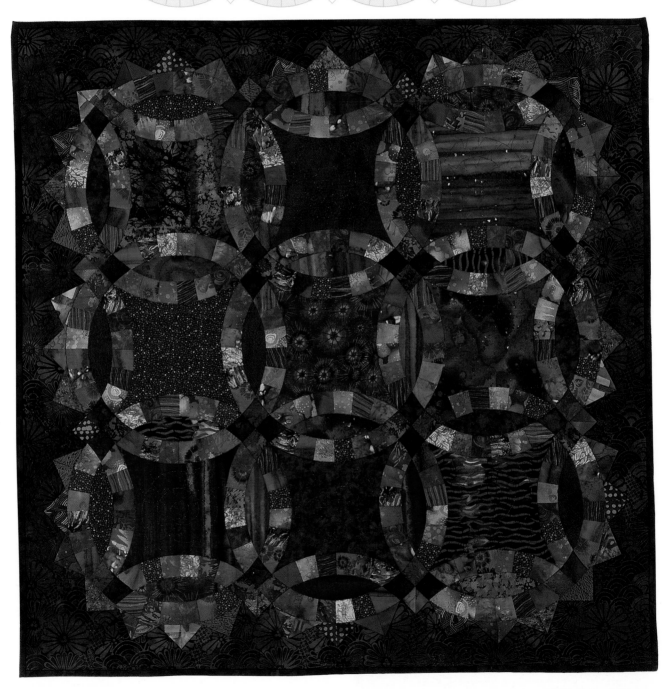

Technique: Scrappy Prairie Points

Finished size: 43" square

Double Wedding Ring Quilts: Coming Full Circle – Susan L. Stein

Fabrics and Supplies*

Assorted scraps or quarter-yards of fabric for wedges and end pieces (I used 18 different fabrics for the wedges and end pieces in my quilt.)

¼ yard each of two fabrics for corner squares

Nine 12" squares of darker-value fabric for large background pieces and melons

Assorted scraps or quarter-yards of contrasting-color fabric for Prairie Points (I used 10 different fabrics for the Prairie Points in my quilt.)

1¼ yards of fabric for border

⅜ yard of fabric for binding

Walking or even-feed foot for machine-guided quilting

Darning foot for free-motion quilting

*See Resources, pages 94-95

Cut

A total of 192 *wedges* and 96 *end pieces,* layering four or five wedge and end piece fabrics

Note: Cut some extra wedges and end pieces to give yourself more options for combining colors and prints around the edges of the rings.

24 *corner squares* each from the two fabrics for corner squares

Layer four or five 12" background squares at a time and cut 9 *background* large pieces and 24 melons

Forty-eight 4" *squares* from the scrap fabrics for Prairie Points

Piecing the Rings

■ Sew the wedges into pairs and then sew the pairs together for each arc, making sure the colors contrast with each other as you combine the various scrap fabrics.

■ Sew the end pieces onto the arcs, making sure that you do not repeat a fabric, and press. Add corner squares to one half of the pieced arcs.

■ Sew the 24 melon units, referring to the photos and instructions on pages 11-13 for "Piecing the Melon Units," and varying the fabrics in the arcs to maintain the scrap look. Press the melon units.

■ Assemble the 9 rings, see "Joining the Rings" on page 12. Lay the elements of each row on a design wall or next to your sewing machine to keep them in order as you sew, and take just one background piece and its pieced melons to the sewing machine at a time. Press the joined rings.

■ Turn under and baste ¼" on the edges of the rings, rounding out the four outer pairs of corner squares.

Adding the Prairie Points and Border

■ Tape the border fabric to a table and lay the rings at the center.

50 Fold the squares of fabric for the Prairie Points in half crosswise, and press. Bring the two folded edges together forming a triangle with folds at the middle. Press the prepared Prairie Points.

Note: When choosing fabrics for a scrap quilt that will be predominantly one color, make sure to include light, medium, and dark values, and make sure that the prints vary in scale.

■ Place a Prairie Point under the edge of the rings, matching the folds in the center of the Prairie Point to the center seam of an arc. Make sure that the raw edges of the Prairie Point extend ¼" under the basted edge of the ring. Pin securely.

■ Referring to the photo on page 72, position two more Prairie Points on either side of the first one, matching the folds in the center of each Prairie Point to the seam lines of the arc. Repeat these two steps all the way around the edges of the rings. Pin securely.

■ Place Prairie Points under the inside corners and at the outside corners of the joined rings, making sure all the points are even. Pin them in place securely.

■ Hang the quilt top on a design wall to check the placement of the Prairie Points. Check for a good level of color contrast between the rings and the points, and change positions of points, if desired.

■ Set your machine to a blind-hem stitch. Machine appliqué the rings to the border fabric, sewing through the Prairie Points at the same time, and referring to "Machine Appliquéing the Border" on page 13. Trim away the border fabric underneath the joined rings, leaving a ¼" seam allowance. Also trim the excess fabric from the Prairie Points at the inner corners of the quilt.

■ Press the completed quilt top.

Machine Quilting

■ Layer the backing, batting, and quilt top, and baste the layers together with thread or safety pins.

■ Using a walking or even-feed foot on your sewing machine, quilt in the seam lines of the rings.

51 Prairie Points are tucked under the edges of the rings and the quilting in the border echoes the points. Quilt ⅜" to ¾" outside the points, parallel to the edges. Then quilt another line echoing the first, but vary the distance between the two lines as you stitch.

■ In the border corners, quilt two more lines, referring to the photo on page 72.

■ Change to a darning foot and lower or cover the feed dogs on your sewing machine. In the large background pieces, free-motion quilt a spiral, and then reverse the direction of stitching to add thorns.

52 More "prickly" points are quilted in the large background pieces.

Finishing

■ Trim the backing fabric and batting to ¼" from the edges of the quilt top. Cut five 2½" x 42" binding strips and bind the quilt, referring to "Attaching the Binding" on page 14.

■ Add a straight casing to the top edge of the back side of the quilt, referring to "Adding a Casing" on page 14.

Rings Around the Posies

Collect some luminous ribbons and your favorite silk flowers for embellishing this fun quilt. After I pieced this quilt top, the quilting and embellishment were done by art quilter, Elizabeth Palmer-Spilker, who is always ready for an adventure. Have fun creating your own garden of delights with colorful silk ribbons and flowers.

Technique: Ribbon-and-silk flowers

Finished size: 42" x 53"

Fabrics and Supplies*

⅓ yard each of six fabrics for wedges and end pieces or
  one bundle of 8 hand-dyed fat quarters ¼ yard each
  of two fabrics for corner squares (included in a
  hand-dyed bundle)

1 yard of fabric for background

1⅝ yards of fabric for border

⅜ yard of fabric for binding

16 yards of ½"-wide nylon organdy ribbon

12 silk flowers   12 buttons or beads

Walking or even-feed for machine-guided quilting

Darning foot for free-motion quilting

*See Resources, pages 94-95

Cut

62 *wedges* each from four of the arc fabrics (values #3
  through #6 from a hand-dyed bundle)

62 *end pieces* each from two of the arc fabrics (values #2
  and #7 from a hand-dyed bundle)

31 *corner squares* each from the corner square fabrics
  (values #1 and #8 from a hand-dyed bundle)

12 *background* large pieces and 31 *melons* from the background fabric

Piecing the Rings

■ Sew the 31 melon units. Lay the pieced melon units
and the large background pieces on a design wall in the
arrangement specified in the project instructions. Then
follow these steps to join the rings together.

■ To sew the melon units to the large background
pieces, begin by finger creasing the center points on the
four curved edges on a large background piece. Match
and pin the center seam of a pieced arc in a melon unit
to a center point on the large background piece.

■ Place another pin ¼" in from the point of the large
background piece; then insert the pin into the seam
between the end piece and corner square of the pieced
arc underneath. Pinch the fabrics together on the pin and
then anchor the pin securely in the fabrics. Repeat this
process at the other point of the large background piece.

Note: The corner squares will be left hanging free. Sew
this seam with the large background piece on top,
backstitching at both ends.

■ Continue to add complete melons to the sides of the
large background pieces as needed for your project,
making sure there are no two corner squares touching
that are the same fabric. Press the seam allowances
toward the background pieces.

■ Sew the corner squares together to complete the
rings, beginning at the raw edges and backstitching at
the end of the seam, and press.

■ To join the rows of pieced rings together, start by
sewing the middle ring in each row together, and work
outward in both directions from there. When you have
joined the rows of rings, go back and sew all of the
pairs of corner squares together. When sewing the corner squares together on the outside edges, backstitch at
the raw edges so the seam allowances remain free for
sewing the rings to the border. Press the seam
allowances toward the background.

■ Turn under and baste ¼" on the edges of the rings,
rounding out the four outer pairs of corner squares.

Adding the Border

■ Set your sewing machine for a blind-hem stitch
with a short stitch length and narrow zigzag width.
Lay the rings on the border fabric and pin securely.

■ Sew the rings to the border, referring to "Machine
Appliquéing the Border" on page 13. Trim away the
border fabric underneath the joined rings leaving a ¼"
seam allowance.

■ Trim the outer edges of the border fabric so they are
equal in width on all sides of the quilt top. Press the
completed quilt top.

Machine Quilting

■ Layer the backing, batting, and quilt top, and baste
the layers together with thread or rust-proof safety pins.

■ Using a walking or even-feed foot on your sewing
machine, quilt in the seam lines of the rings.

■ Change to a darning foot, and lower or cover the
feed dogs on your sewing machine. Free-motion

quilt a loopy, freehand design in the large background pieces to echo the ribbon loops and stabilize the layers of the quilt. Begin by drawing a design on a piece of tracing paper and pinning it to the background area. Quilt the design through the paper, removing and discarding the paper after your stitching is complete.

Adding the Ribbon and Silk Flowers

■ Cut four 12" lengths of ribbon. Thread a hand-sewing needle and knot the thread. Insert the needle through both ends of one piece of ribbon, and tack the ends together creating a loop. Insert the needle through the mid-point of the ribbon loop and tack the ribbon to the ends of the ribbon creating a double loop. Repeat with the other three pieces.

■ Tack the four looped pieces together to create a background unit to go behind each flower. Make a total of 12 of these units.

■ Take the silk flowers apart and remove any plastic pieces. Arrange the leaves underneath and the petals on top of the ribbon loop unit on each large background piece and tack them in place by machine, using a few short satin stitches. Cover this stitching by sewing a bead or button at the center of each flower.

53 The ribbon loops are echoed in the loopy quilting around the silk flowers.

Finishing

■ Trim the backing fabric and batting to ¼" from the edges of the quilt top.

■ Cut five 2½" x 42" binding strips and bind the quilt, referring to "Attaching the Binding" on page 14.

■ Add a casing to the top edge of the back side of the quilt, referring to "Adding a Casing" on page 14.

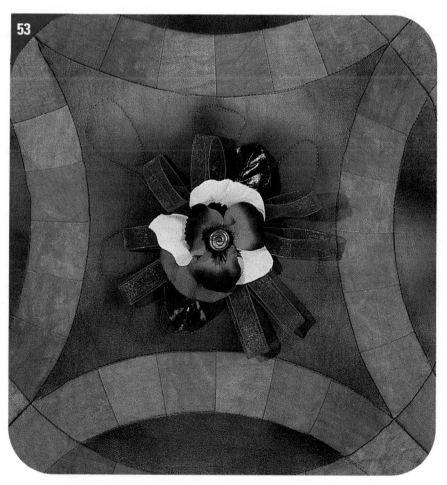

Double Wedding Ring Quilts: Coming Full Circle – Susan L. Stein

Falling Leaves & Leaf Dance

*Collect your favorite fall prints or hand-dyed fabrics and have fun making
an autumn quilt to decorate a wall, table, or door. Raw edges on the leaves
look natural and make this project quick and easy to finish. The leaves are
held in place only by the quilting, allowing the edges to curl slightly.*

Technique:
Raw-edged leaves

FALLING LEAVES: Finished size: 18" x 57"

LEAF DANCE: Finished size: 18" x 60"

Double Wedding Ring Quilts: Coming Full Circle – Susan L. Stein

Note: These directions apply to either quilt.

Fabrics and Supplies*

¼ yard each of eight fabrics for wedges, end pieces, and corner squares, or a hand-dyed bundle of eight fat quarters

⅔ yard of fabric for background

1 yard of fabric for border

⅓ yard of fabric for binding

¼ yard each of eight leaf fabrics (Choose fabrics with some color on the back side so they won't look white when the raw edges curl.)

Glue stick

Walking or even-feed foot for machine-guided quilting

*See Resources, pages 94-95

Cut

32 *wedges* each from four colors of fabric

32 *end pieces* each from two colors of fabric

16 *corner squares* each from two colors of fabric

16 *melons* and 5 *large background* pieces from the background fabric.

23 *leaves* using the patterns on page 80 and 81.

Piecing the Rings

■ Sew the 16 melon units, referring to the photos and instructions on pages 11-13 for "Piecing the Melon Units," and press.

■ Assemble 5 rings, referring to "Joining the Rings" on page 12. Lay the elements of each row on a design wall or next to your sewing machine to keep them in order and take just one background piece and its pieced melons to the sewing machine at a time. Press the joined rings.

■ Turn under and baste ¼" on the edges of the rings, rounding out the four outer pairs of corner squares.

Adding the Border

■ Cut the border fabric into two ½-yard pieces and sew them end-to-end. Press the seam open.

■ Set your machine to a blind-hem stitch. Lay the rings on the border fabric and pin them in place.

■ Machine appliqué the rings to the border, referring to "Machine Appliquéing the Border" on page 13.

■ Trim away the border fabric underneath the joined rings, leaving a ¼" seam allowance.

■ Trim the outer edges of the border fabric so they are equal in width on all sides of the quilt top. Press the completed quilt top.

Adding the Leaves

■ Hang the quilt top on a design wall and arrange the leaves evenly on top.

■ When you are happy with your leaf placements, use a glue-stick to stick them very lightly in place. It may seem tempting to fuse the leaves in place, but they will look more natural if they are not stiff and tightly adhered to the quilt top along the edges of the leaves.

Machine Quilting

■ Layer the backing, batting, and quilt top, and baste the layers together with thread or rust-proof pins.

■ Using a walking or even-feed foot on your sewing machine, quilt straight horizontal lines across the quilt by eye at approximately 2" intervals, catching the leaves as you stitch.

■ Then quilt more horizontal lines between your previous lines of stitching; this time, start each line of stitching from the opposite edge, to keep the top layer of the quilt from shifting. Make these lines slightly wavy to add visual interest.

■ Finally, quilt more horizontal lines of stitching between each of your previous lines, resulting in a pattern of horizontal lines at approximately ½" intervals across the entire quilt. You will notice that the points of the leaves will curl a bit, as real leaves do, but they will be held securely in place by the quilting lines.

54a & 54b The quilting extends from one side to the other, adding texture as well as holding the leaves.

Finishing

■ Trim the backing fabric and batting even with the edges of the quilt top.

■ Cut four 2" x 42" binding strips and bind the quilt, referring to "Attaching the Binding" on page 14.

■ Add a casing to the top edge of the back side of the quilt. To make a casing for displaying a straight-edged wall quilt, start with a 9" x 42" strip of fabric. Trim the strip to the width of the quilt and hem under 1" at the short ends. Fold the strip in half lengthwise, wrong sides together. Pin and baste the raw edges to the top of the quilt backing, before you stitch the binding to the backing fabric. Hand sew the bottom fold of the casing to the backing; then sew the binding in place, enclosing the top edge of the casing.

Leaves appear in both
FALLING LEAVES and LEAF DANCE

No seam allowances are needed for
raw-edged leaves.

54a

Leaves appear in both
FALLING LEAVES and LEAF DANCE

No seam allowances are needed for
raw-edged leaves.

Double Wedding Ring Quilts: Coming Full Circle – Susan L. Stein

Fruit Basket Upset

*Many years ago, after seeing a weaving exhibit of thick, wonderfully textured pieces,
I decided that I wanted to add more texture to my quilts. Raw-edge appliqué and piecing
provide great visual interest, and if sewn with care, they will last as long as traditional
patchwork and appliqué. For this quilt, I chose hand-dyed fabric for the rings and
overdyed decorator prints for the background and border fabrics.*

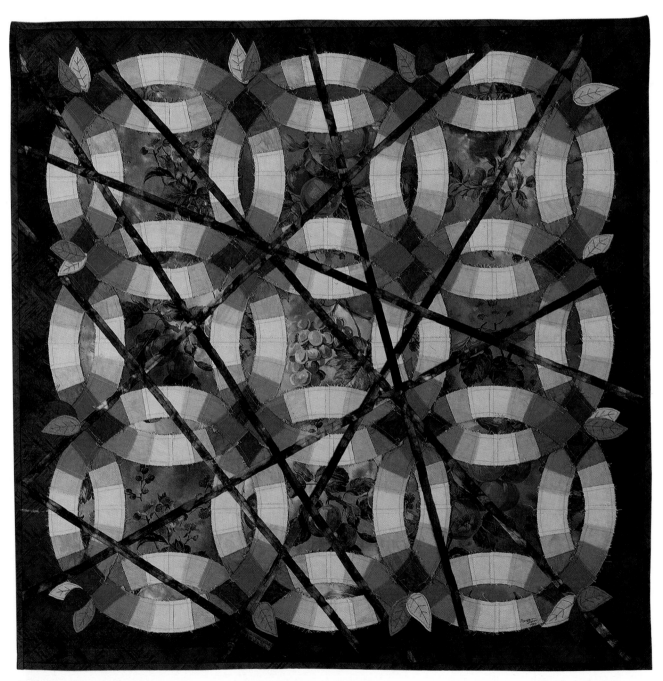

Technique: Raw-edged piecing

Finished size: 41" square

Double Wedding Ring Quilts: Coming Full Circle – Susan L. Stein

Fabrics and Supplies*

1/3 yard each of eight print fabrics or one bundle of eight hand-dyed fat quarters (19" squares) for wedges, end pieces, and corner squares

1 yard of fabric for background

1 1/4 yards of fabric for border

3/8 yard of fabric for binding

10 yards of hand-dyed rayon seam tape or silk ribbon

Glue stick & chalk pencil

Walking or even-feed foot for machine-guided quilting

Darning foot for free-motion quilting

*See Resources, pages 94-95

Note: To create an even more frayed look in raw-edged piecing, choose more loosely woven cotton broadcloth rather than tightly woven batiks and pima cottons.

Cut

48 *wedges* each from four colors of fabric

48 *end pieces* each from two colors of fabric

24 *corner squares* each from two colors of fabric

9 *background* large pieces and 24 *melons* from the background fabric

Piecing the Rings

■ Sew the 24 melon units, referring to the photos and instructions on pages 11-13 for "Piecing the Melon Units." Choose a thread color carefully since it will show on the outside of the quilt. If you are using print fabrics, turn the fabric over and sew with the wrong side as the front. Be sure to use a firm stitch that will allow the fabric to fray attractively but will hold the seams securely. Press the melon units. *Note:* Remember that the viewer will see the seams so this is the time to fix twisted seam allowances and keep everything neat. After the quilting is done you can "mess up" the seam allowances and fray them more, if you like.

■ Assemble the 9 rings, referring to "Joining the Rings" on page 12, keeping in mind that the seams should show on the right side of the finished quilt. Lay the elements of each row on a design wall or next to your sewing machine to keep them in order as you sew, and take just one background piece and its pieced melons to the sewing machine at a time. Press the joined rings. *Note:* If the wrong side of your background fabric

Double Wedding Ring Quilts: Coming Full Circle – Susan L. Stein

is attractive, make a few "intentional mistakes" in the way you place the right and wrong sides of the large background pieces and/or melons.

Adding the Border

■ Cut four 5" x 42" strips of border fabric on the lengthwise grain. Lay the joined rings on the strips of border fabric without turning under the edges of the rings and match the centers of the border strips with the centers of the rings. Make sure that the inner corners of the rings extend over the edge of the strips by ¼". Pin the joined rings to the border strips securely.

■ Straight stitch ¼" in from the raw outer edges of the joined rings, beginning and ending with backstitching at the seam between the corner squares. Trim the border fabric away underneath the rings leaving a ¼" seam allowance.

■ Miter the border corner seams by folding one border strip over the adjacent border strip at a 45-degree angle and using blind-hem appliqué to stitch the fold in place. Trim the mitered seam allowances to ¼".

Machine Quilting

■ Layer the backing, batting, and quilt top, and baste the layers together with thread or rust-proof safety pins.

■ Using a chalk pencil and yardstick, draw lines across the quilt top. Make sure there are enough evenly spaced lines so that the quilt will lie flat when it is finished. Lay lengths of ribbon or seam tape over the lines. Using a walking or even-feed foot on your sewing machine, topstitch through the middle of the tape or ribbon so the edges pop up.

55 Rayon twill tape is stitched down the center to raise the edges of the tape and create texture. Refer to photograph on page 83.

■ Cut out a selection of free-form leaves by eye, referring to the photo on page 82 for guidance. Using a glue stick, glue the leaves to the quilt top in an arrangement that pleases you.

■ Change to a darning foot on your sewing machine and drop or cover the feed dogs. Using a short stitch length for greater durability, topstitch the leaves ⅛" from the raw edges, and add veins to the leaves.

56 Raw-edged free-form leaves are added to the outer edges of the rings for extra interest.

Finishing

■ Trim the backing fabric and batting to ¼" from the edges of the quilt top.

■ Cut five 2½" x 42" binding strips and bind the quilt, capturing the ends of the tape or ribbon, referring to "Attaching the Binding" on page 14. Shake the quilt and brush the raw edges to fray the fabrics.

■ Add a casing to the top edge of the back side of the quilt. To make a casing for displaying a straight-edged wall quilt, start with a 9" x 42" strip of fabric. Trim the strip to the width of the quilt and hem under 1" at the short ends. Fold the strip in half lengthwise, wrong sides together. Pin and baste the raw edges to the top of the quilt backing, before you stitch the binding to the backing fabric. Hand sew the bottom fold of the casing to the backing; then sew the binding in place, enclosing the top edge of the casing.

Natural Rhythms

This project is the place to use up small pieces of hand-dyed fabric that are too precious to throw away, a selection of mail-order swatches, or fabrics from a dyeing workshop. Irregular scraps are fine because this quilt allows you to mix and match the wedges as you go along. Use as many colors and values as you like, making sure that they contrast with the border and background fabrics.

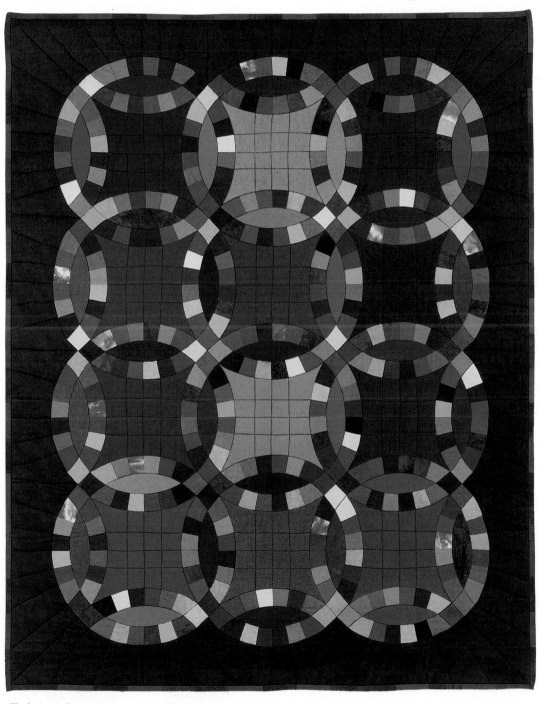

Technique: Creating a scrap look with solids   Finished size: Approximately 43" x 54"

Double Wedding Ring Quilts: Coming Full Circle – Susan L. Stein

Fabrics and Supplies

Approximately 2 yards total of small pieces of hand dyed or other solid-color fabrics in many colors for pieced arcs

¼ yard each of two fabrics for corner squares

12" squares of twelve fabrics for large background pieces and melons

1⅔ yards of fabric for border

1⅔ yards fabric for backing

¼ yard each of 4 fabrics for pieced binding

Walking or even-feed foot for machine-guided quilting

Cut

A total of 248 *wedges* by placing four scraps of fabric on top of each other, disregarding the unmatched edges. Lay the wedge template on top and cut out as many stacks of wedges as possible, throwing away any partial pieces. Continue by layering four more scraps of fabric each time.

Using scraps, cut out 124 *end pieces*. Remember when you are using printed fabrics, you will need to cut 62 *end pieces* with the right side of the fabric facing up, and 62 *end pieces* with the wrong side of the fabric facing up

31 *corner squares* each from the two fabrics for corner squares

12 *background* large pieces and 31 *melons* from the twelve 12" squares

Piecing the Rings

■ Sew the 31 melon units, referring to the photos and instructions on pages 11-13 for "Piecing the Melon Units," and press. As you piece the arcs, mix the wedge colors so each arc is different, and add a different end piece at the ends of each arc. Press the melon units.

■ Assemble the 12 rings, referring to "Joining the Rings" on page 12. Lay the elements of each row on a design wall or next to your sewing machine to keep them in order as you sew and take just one background piece and its pieced melons to the sewing machine at a time. Press the joined rings.

■ Turn under and baste ¼" on the edges of the rings, rounding out the four outer pairs of corner squares.

Adding the Border

■ Set your sewing machine for a blind-hem stitch with a short stitch length and narrow zigzag width. Lay the rings on the border fabric and pin them in place securely.

■ Sew the rings to the border, referring to "Machine Appliquéing the Border" on page 13. Trim away the border fabric underneath the joined rings, leaving a ¼" seam allowance.

■ Trim the outer edges of the border fabric so they are equal in width on all sides of the quilt top. Press the completed quilt top.

Machine Quilting

■ Layer the backing, batting, and quilt top, and baste the layers together with thread or rust-proof safety pins.

■ Using a walking or even-feed foot on your sewing machine, quilt in the seam lines of the rings.

■ Quilt slightly curved lines across the background pieces from wedge seam to wedge seam.

57 Quilting is simple with slightly curved lines filling the background pieces.

■ Quilt across the borders, starting at the wedge seams, and maintaining the angle of the seams. Use only your eyes to gauge the lines. Curves complement the rings better than rigid straight lines.

58 The border quilting lines extend outward from the seam lines of the rings.

Finishing

■ Trim the backing fabric and batting to ¼" from the edges of the quilt top.

■ Cut a 3" x 42" binding strip from each of the four binding fabrics and sew them side by side. Press the seam allowances open.

■ Cut 2½"-wide slices from the strip set and sew them end-to-end to make the pieced binding strip. Fold the pieced binding strip in half lengthwise with wrong sides together, and press.

■ Bind the quilt, referring to "Attaching the Binding" on page 14.

■ Add a casing to the top edge of the back side of the quilt, referring to "Adding a Casing" on page 14.

I cut the wedges for my quilt and left them overnight on a table in front of an open window. In the early morning, a powerful gust of wind blew them all over the house where they showed up for weeks afterward, hiding under beds and behind furniture!

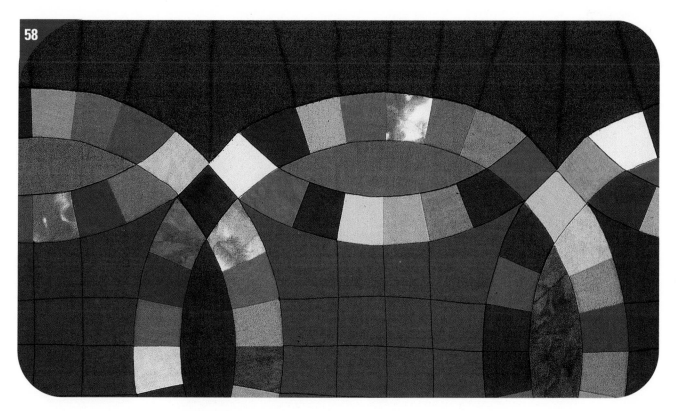

Romancing the Ring

Rubber stamps are fun to play with, and they are readily available at large fabric and decorating stores. For this quilt, any designs that will fit into the large background areas and the melons will work well. Choose a fabric paint that matches one of your fabrics, gather some supplies from around the house, and you're ready to go.

Technique: Rubber stamped background fabric

Finished size: Approximately 43" square (61" point-to-point)

Double Wedding Ring Quilts: Coming Full Circle – Susan L. Stein

Fabrics and Supplies*

1 yard of print fabric for one-piece arcs

¼ yard each of two fabrics for corner squares

1 yard of light-value, tightly woven fabric with smooth surface for stamping

1¼ yards of fabric for border

½ yard of fabric for binding

Textile paint in a color to match the ring or border fabric

1"-wide sponge brush for stamping designs on fabric

Tiny paint brush to fix mistakes

Sponge stamps with designs that fit melons and large background pieces

Plastic garbage bag

Paper towels

2⅓ yards of 1"-wide twill tape

2⅓ yards of ½"-wide hook and loop tape

Foam core board

Walking or even-feed foot for machine-guided quilting

Darning foot for free-motion quilting

*See Resources, pages 94-95

Cut

48 *one-piece arcs* from the print fabrics

24 *corner squares* each from the two fabrics for corner squares

24 *melons* and 9 *large background* pieces

Note: Cut out some extra melons and large background pieces to test the paint, stamps, and design placements, and to allow for discarding any that do not please you.

Stamping the Background Fabric

■ You can use several small stamps in each area. You might even want to stamp the borders.

■ Lay out the plastic garbage bag on a table; if there are creases in the plastic bag, tape the edges to the table.

CAUTION! Be sure to work in a well-ventilated area and avoid inhaling paint fumes as you stamp the fabric.

■ Gather the textile paints, sponge, paint brushes, paper towels, cut fabric pieces, and rubber stamps in your work area. If necessary, you can cut a stamp in half or trim away a small part of it to fit the melon

shape. Pour some paint into a small container so you can dip the sponge brush into it.

■ Lay out several fabric pieces on the garbage bag. Dip the sponge brush into the textile paint, wiping the brush on the side of the container lightly to remove any excess paint.

■ Using a dabbing motion, brush paint onto the surface of the rubber stamp until there is an even layer of paint on all of the raised surfaces. Do not use a brushing motion which will leave lines in the painted image on the fabric.

■ Lay the rubber stamp face down on one of the fabric pieces and press down firmly on all areas of the stamp.

59 Carefully lift the stamp straight up from the fabric. It will take a bit of practice to learn how much pressure to apply as you stamp designs; too little pressure often creates an imperfect image, while too much can smear the paint.

■ You can fix lightly painted areas by using a tiny paint brush to add paint to the surface of the fabric. And

remember, hand work should show slight imperfections or people will think it is factory-made!

■ Set the painted fabric pieces aside and allow them to dry completely. Wipe up any paint that may have come through onto the plastic garbage bag and continue to stamp more fabric pieces until you have enough good ones for your quilt top.

■ After the paint is dry, heat set it with a dry iron set on "cotton" to make the color permanent. Be careful not to stretch the fabric when you press the pieces.

Piecing the Rings
■ Sew the 24 melon units, referring to the photos and instructions on pages 11-13 for "Piecing the Melon Units," and press.

■ Assemble the 9 rings, referring to "Joining the Rings" on page 12. Lay the elements of each row on a design wall or next to your sewing machine to keep them in order as you sew and take just one background piece and its pieced melons to the sewing machine at a time. Press the joined rings.

■ Turn under and baste ¼" on the edges of the rings, rounding out the four outer pairs of corner squares.

Adding the Border
■ Set your sewing machine for a blind-hem stitch with a short stitch length and narrow zigzag width. Lay the rings on the border fabric and pin them in place securely.

■ Sew the rings to the border, referring to "Machine Appliquéing the Border" on page 13. Trim away the border fabric underneath the joined rings, leaving a ¼" seam allowance.

■ Trim the outer edges of the border fabric so they are equal in width on all sides of the quilt top. Press the completed quilt top.

Machine Quilting
■ Layer the backing, batting, and quilt top, and baste the layers together with thread or rust-proof safety pins.

■ Using a walking or even-feed foot on your sewing machine, quilt in the seam lines of the rings

■ Change to a darning foot and lower or cover the feed dogs on your sewing machine. Stipple quilt the borders.

Finishing
■ Trim the backing fabric and batting to ¼" from the edges of the quilt top.

■ Cut five 2½" x 42" binding strips and bind the quilt, referring to "Attaching the Binding" on page 14.

■ To hang the quilt on point, sew the loop half of the hook and loop tape along both sides, to the center of the twill tape. Cut the tape in half and sew it by hand to the two top edges of the quilt, just under the binding. Do not sew the hook and loop tape directly to the quilt as it may discolor the fabrics.

■ Glue the hook half of the hook and loop tape to a piece of foam core board, cut into a triangle that is the size of the top half of the quilt, minus 1" on each side. Attach a picture hook to the back side of the foam core board for hanging. Press the quilt to the foam core to display it.

Double Wedding Ring Pattern

Double Wedding Ring
15" Pattern

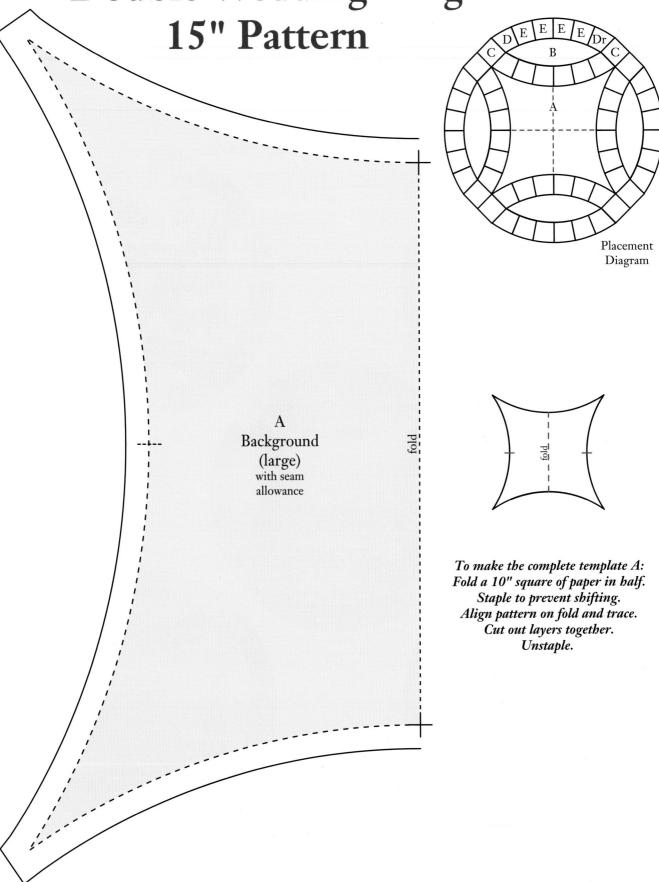

Placement
Diagram

A
Background
(large)
with seam
allowance

fold

fold

To make the complete template A:
Fold a 10" square of paper in half.
Staple to prevent shifting.
Align pattern on fold and trace.
Cut out layers together.
Unstaple.

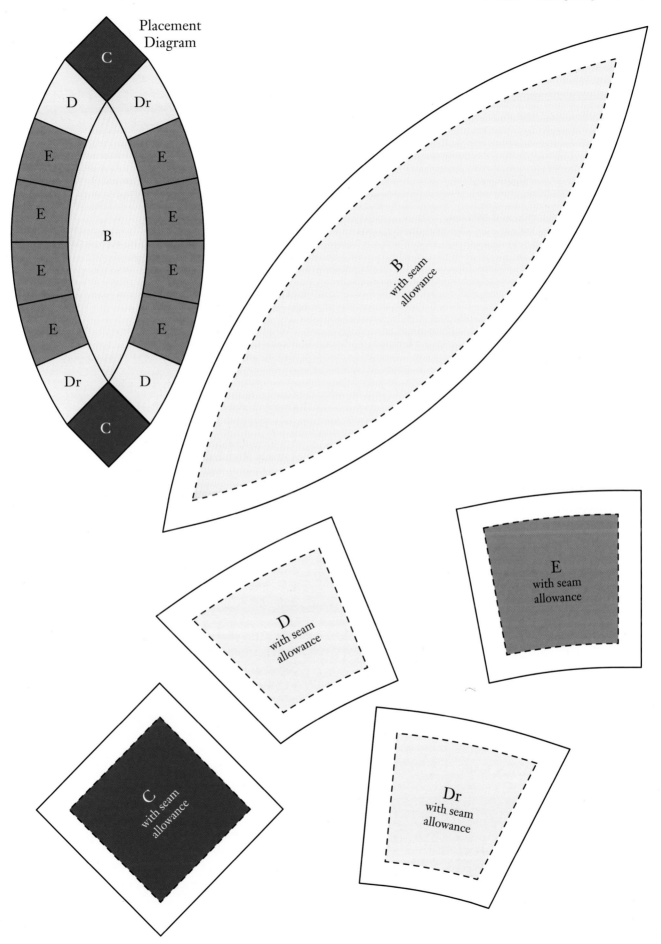

Placement Diagram

C

D   Dr

E   E

E   E

B

E   E

E   E

E   E

Dr   D

C

B
with seam
allowance

D
with seam
allowance

E
with seam
allowance

C
with seam
allowance

Dr
with seam
allowance

Resources

Listed here are the author's personal preferences and resources for materials and information included in this book. Specific projects in which items are used or referenced are shown in bold capital letters.

Fabrics

PHANTOM RINGS
Hand-dyed cotton, silk, and threads
Artfabrik by Laura Wasilowski and Melody Johnson
664 W. Main St., Cary IL 60013
847-639-5966; www.artfabrik.com

RING AROUND THE POSIES (Background)
One yard "atmospheric" dyed pieces
Artspoken Yardage by Marit Lee Kucera
30 South St. Albans St. #5, St. Paul, MN 55105
651-222-2483

AFTERGLOW (Arcs)
Hand-dyed cotton and silk
Diane Bartels
5246 Piper Road, Mound, MN 55364
(952) 472-4154; dibartels@ispchannel.com

FLOWER CROSSINGS
HINT OF PASSION (Fossil Fern collection)
RIVER OF GOLD (Arcs)
Fabrics for quiltmaking
Benartex, Inc.
1460 Broadway, 8th Floor, New York, NY 10036
(212) 840-3250; www.benartex.com

CLIMBING ROSES (All fabrics)
LEAF DANCE (Rings)
FRUIT BASKET UPSET (Rings)
REFLECTIONS ON A LINE (Rings)
RING AROUND THE POSIES (Rings)
SKY TRAILS (Rings)
TORRID ORCHID (Rings)
Dyed bundles of fabric
Cherrywood Fabrics
PO Box 486, Brainerd, MN 56401
888-298-0967

Fabrics to paint and dye, hand-dyed fabrics
Lunn Fabrics
317 E. Main St., Lancaster, OH 43130
614-654-2202; www.lunnfabrics.com

AFTERGLOW (Background and melons)
JAPANESE CHRYSANTHEMUMS (Background)
Overdyed kimono silks
Laura Murray
5021 15th Ave. S., Minneapolis, MN 55417
612-825-1209; LMurray128@aol.com

LAYERED ILLUSIONS (Arcs)
NASTURTIUMS (Arcs)
Bundles of fabric in dyed gradations
Primrose Gradations
PO Box 6, Two Harbors, MN 55616-0006
888-Dye-Arts; www.dyearts.com

REFLECTIONS ON A LINE (Background)
FRUIT BASKET UPSET (Background and border)
Overdyed decorator prints
Wendy Richardson
8009 Florida Ave. N.
Brooklyn Park, MN 55445-2629
763-566-3339; WendyRQTS@aol.com

JAPANESE CHRYSANTHEMUMS (One-piece rings)
Hand-dyed cotton fabric
Judy Robertson
P.O. Box 83, Bow, WA 98232
360-766-4030

SKY TRAILS (Background)
Hand-painted cottons
Skydyes by Mickey Lawler
PO Box 370116, West Hartford, CT 06137-0116

Foil, Surface Design, Dyes, and Paints

Assortments of 9" x 12" sheets of foil
Colorful Quilts & Textiles, Inc.
2817 North Hamline Ave., Roseville, MN 55113
651-628-9664

Catalog of everything you need for surface design, plus good how-to information
Dharma Trading Co.
PO Box 150916, San Rafael, CA 94915
800-542-5227; www.dharmatrading.com

Double Wedding Ring Quilts: Coming Full Circle – Susan L. Stein

LILIANNA
Pebco™ transparent Setacolor™ fabric paints

Dyes and paints
Pro Chemical and Dye
PO Box 14, Somerset, MA 02726
800-2-BUY-DYE; www.prochemical.com

ROMANCING THE RING (Wallpaper Roses stamp set)
Rubber Stamps
Rubber Stampede

200-foot rolls and sample packs of craft foil
Screen-Trans Development Corp.
100 Grand St., Moonachie, NJ 07074
201-933-7800

Notions
REFLECTIONS ON A LINE
Fusible web
Steam-a-Seam II™

LILIANNA
Fusible woven cotton interfacing
Shape-Flex™ by Stacy

FRUIT BASKET UPSET
Hand-dyed rayon seam tape
Wendy Richardson
8009 Florida Ave. N.
Brooklyn Park, MN 55445-2629
763-566-3339; WendyRQTS@aol.com

ROMANCING THE RING
Hook and Loop Tape
Velcro™

REFLECTIONS ON A LINE
Piping
Maxi Piping™ by Wrights

Templates
Acrylic template sets and instructional videos by
Sharlene Jorgenson for Double Wedding Ring and
other patterns.
Quilting From the Heartland
PO Box 610 , Starbuck, MN 56381
800-637-2541; www.qheartland.com

Threads
FLOWER CROSSINGS (Stems)
#12 hand-dyed perle cotton thread

HINT OF PASSION
SKY TRAILS (Beading threads)
Nymo™
Silamide™

FLOWER CROSSINGS (Leaves – rayon thread)
RINGS ON SQUARES (Metallic™ and Sliver™)
Sulky Threads

Books
American Quilter's Society. *Double Wedding Ring Quilts: New Quilts from an Old Favorite*. 1994.

Bishop, Robert. *The Romance of Double Wedding Ring Quilts*. E. P. Dutton. 1989.

REFLECTIONS ON A LINE
Dunnewold, Jane. *Complex Cloth, A Comprehensive Guide to Surface Design*. Fiber Studio Press. 1996.

TORRID ORCHID
Holmberg, Nannette. *Variations in Chenille*. That Patchwork Place. 1997.

SKY TRAILS
Lawler, Mickey. *Skydyes, A Visual Guide to Fabric Painting*. C & T Publishing. 1999.

LILIANNA
Porcella, Yvonne. *Colors Changing Hue*. C & T Publishing. 1994.

CLIMBING ROSES
Sudo, Kumiko. *Fabled Flowers: Innovative Quilt Patterns Inspired by Japanese Sashiko and Origami Traditions*. Quilt Digest. 1996.

Townswick, Jane. *Artful Appliqué The Easy Way*. Martingale & Co., Inc. 2000.

OTHER AQS BOOKS

This is only a small selection of the books available from the American Quilter's Society. AQS books are known worldwide for timely topics, clear writing, beautiful color photos, and accurate illustrations and patterns. The following books are available from your local bookseller, quilt shop, or the public library.

#5855   US $22.95

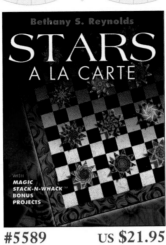

#5589   US $21.95

#5754   US $19.95

#5850   US $21.95

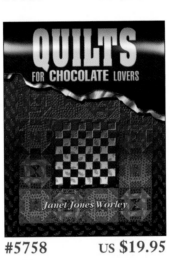

#5758   US $19.95

#5705   US $22.95

#5755   US $21.95

#5844   US $21.95

#5853   US $18.95

Look for these books nationally or call 1-800-626-5420